The Sal

T0208502

V

# The Salaried Masses

## Duty and Distraction in Weimar Germany

◆

### SIEGFRIED KRACAUER

Translated by Quintin Hoare

and with an Introduction
by Inka Mülder-Bach

**VERSO**
London • New York

First published by Verso 1998
This edition © Verso 1998
Translation © Quintin Hoare 1998
Introduction © Inka Mülder-Bach 1998
First published as *Die Angestellten. Aus dem neuesten Deutschland*, serial publication
in *Frankfurter Zeitung* 1929; first published in book form by Societäts-Verlag,
Frankfurt am Main 1930, © Suhrkamp Verlag, Frankfurt am Main 1971,
in Siegfried Kracauer, *Schriften*, Volume 1
Walter Benjamin, 'Ein Aussenseiter macht sich bemerkbar', in
*Gesammelte Schriften*, Volume 3

**Verso**
UK: 6 Meard Street, London W1V 3HR
USA: 180 Varick Street, New York NY 10014–4606

Verso is the imprint of New Left Books

ISBN 978-1-85984-187-7

**British Library Cataloguing in Publication Data**
A catalogue record for this book is available from the British Library

**Library of Congress Cataloging-in-Publication Data**
A catalog record for this book is available from the Library of Congress

Typeset by SetSystems Ltd, Saffron Walden, Essex
Printed by Biddles Ltd, Guildford and King's Lynn

# Contents

Introduction *by Inka Mülder-Bach*     1

Preface     25
Unknown territory     28
Selection     33
Short break for ventilation     40
Enterprise within the enterprise     47
Alas, so soon!     53
Repair shop     60
A few choice specimens     68
Refined informality     74
Among neighbours     81
Shelter for the homeless     88
Seen from above     96
Dear colleagues, ladies and gentlemen!     102

Appendices     107
A. 'An outsider attracts attention'
    *by Walter Benjamin*     109
B. Chronology     115
C. Bibliography     117

Translator's note     121

# Introduction
*Inka Mülder-Bach*

In the Introduction to his last, posthumously published book *History. The Last Things Before the Last* (1969), Siegfried Kracauer formulates a *summa* of his intellectual existence. The discovery of the hidden connection between his interest in history and his interest in the photographic media also reveals to him the central intention that guided his thought for half a century: 'at long last all my main efforts, so incoherent on the surface, fall into line – they all have served, and continue to serve, a single purpose: the rehabilitation of objectives and modes of being which still lack a name and hence are overlooked or misjudged.'[1] Kracauer particularly mentions in this connection two books from his Weimar period: the novel *Ginster* (1928) and the study *Die Angestellten* [*The Salaried Masses*] (1930). Like *Theory of Film* (1960) and *History*, they survey regions of reality 'which despite all that has been written about them are still largely *terra incognita*'.[2]

When Kracauer wrote these lines at the beginning of the 1960s, the readership that might have understood them no longer existed – and did not yet exist anew. The essays and books written before his exile from Germany had never become known in the English-speaking countries and had fallen into oblivion in Germany; the books of his American exile met largely with misunderstanding or perplexed silence. The latter circumstance is directly related to the former. For just as Kracauer in the Introduction to *History* reverts directly to expressions coined in the context of his early writings, so his later work as a whole can be understood only against the background of the traditions, themes and figures of thought of his Weimar texts. A first step in introducing the German writer of the 1920s to an English-speaking public was the recently published translation of the essay collection *The Mass Ornament*.[3] It displays Kracauer as phenomenologist and philosopher of history, as critic of modern literature and film. The present book shows him in a related but somewhat different role: as a sociologist of culture and the quotidian, mapping the *terra incognita* of salaried employees in the last years of the Weimar Republic.


Like almost all his other writings from the Weimar period, *Die Angestell-ten* first appeared (in instalments) in the *feuilleton* – i.e. the cultural section – of the prestigious *Frankfurter Zeitung*. Following studies in architecture, sociology and philosophy, Kracauer worked for this paper from 1921 on – initially as a regular freelance contributor, after 1924 as a full editor, and from 1930 until his February 1933 flight from Nazi Germany as cultural editor for the paper's Berlin pages. From late April to July 1929 Kracauer stayed in Berlin to carry out the research for his study on employees. In October the text was completed, but objections from the paper's editorial board delayed its publication.[4] Due to the support of Benno Reifenberg, the editor of the *feuilleton* section to whom *Die Angestellten* is dedicated, its pre-publication finally went forward in December. 'A sensation has been handed us', Reifenberg wrote to the newspaper's editor-in-chief Heinrich Simon,[5] and the readership's reaction proved him right. In January 1930, the study was published as a book.[6]

Kracauer subtitled the book with a phrase which, with laconic brevity, defines the viewpoint, method and claim of his investigation. What his study aims to be is neither a scientific treatise 'about', nor a literary reportage 'on', the salaried class. Rather Kracauer adopts the role of the ethnologist, who sets off on a sociological 'expedition' to a domestic 'abroad' and reports 'from the newest Germany' (a literal translation of the German original, *Aus dem neuesten Deutschland*) on the salaried employees as if from some exotic foreign land. Kracauer does not let slip the opportunity to juxtapose the 'exoticism' of this world with that of 'primitive tribes at whose habits' the employees 'marvel in films'. The ethnological metaphor, however, is not meant merely ironically but is closely connected with the method and concern of his study. For Kracauer really is setting off. Leaving statistics and learned studies behind, he embarks on an empirical inquiry into the spheres of existence, habits, patterns of thought and manners of speech of salaried employees. He talks to the employees themselves, to union representa-tives and to employers; he visits offices and firms, labour exchanges and Labour Courts, cinemas and places of entertainment; he studies com-pany newspapers, classified advertisements and private correspondence. His procedure has occasionally been compared with the method of 'participant observation' that the Lynds were developing at roughly the same time in their study on Middletown. Yet Kracauer's approach is characterized by a highly self-conscious individualism which resists methodological generalization and crucially involves the *mise en scène* of foreignness and distance as a condition of attention and a medium of knowledge.

The terrain Kracauer seeks to explore, then, is named in the subtitle as 'the newest Germany'. The superlative evokes the sensationalism of contemporary reportage and at the same time ironizes it.[7] For the sensation Kracauer offers us is simply that of daily life: 'normal existence' in its 'imperceptible dreadfulness'. If both aspects – newness and normality – are considered together, the ethnological metaphor acquires a further significance. Kracauer's study is an expedition also in the sense that it not only offers a sociology of salaried employees, but through an analysis of this social stratum's everyday world seeks to discover 'the newest Germany', the most advanced state of economic and socio-cultural modernization. His inquiry thus leads into the heart of the modern large enterprise, which – as an extreme case of economic rationalization – provides a basis for studying the organizational forms that in future will determine the process of production and distribution. And it also leads into the heart of the metropolis Berlin. For just as 'the economic process engendering salaried employees en masse has advanced furthest' in Berlin, so have employees here for the first time become the formative power of the public sphere.

Kracauer compares the life of the employees with the purloined letter in Edgar Allan Poe's famous tale, protected from discovery precisely by being on public display. By wresting it from anonymity and naming it, he places it into a twofold light. On the one hand, he presents the employees as agents and victims of a socio-cultural modernization which has occurred in similar ways in all the advanced capitalist countries of the West. Thus, in reference to this stratum, Kracauer is the first to describe the functional connection between work and leisure, between economic rationalization and the distraction provided by the culture industry; he captures *in statu nascendi* the specific modern process of identity formation, no longer mediated primarily through origin and tradition, but increasingly through secondary and tertiary means of socialization; he describes the new physical mechanisms of selection and standardization, under the pressure of which physiognomies begin to resemble one another and a metropolitan type – uniform in terms of language, clothes and gestures – is formed; he discovers youth as a modern fetish; and he recognizes the increasing importance of women in the world of work and as consumers of mass culture.

In retrospect, however, his study reads not just as a description of the modernization of everyday life, but also as an anticipatory diagnosis of the contradictions, distortions and delusions that the National Socialists were to mobilize a few years later. Below the surface of the international fashion of the weekend the salaried employees cultivated models of self-definition in terms of bureaucratic rank and professional stratum, rooted in specifically German traditions. Indeed, there was no other Western country in which employees, both in their own consciousness and in that of the public, so early played such a central role as in Germany.[8] In no other were they so intensively courted by politics; in no other was the distinction between workers and salaried employees marked so sharply and with such far-reaching consequences. The concept of the 'new middle class' had been coined at the end of the nineteenth century. It defined the employees as the new centre of society and assigned them the function of a buffer against socialist endeavours. The *Angestelltenversicherungsgesetz* of 1911 – which had no equivalent in any other Western country – confirmed this concept by granting them legal privileges in terms of insurance and labour rights and defining them as a higher stratum in relation to the working class. The economic rationalization in the mid-1920s, which also impinged on the former bourgeoisie already dispossessed during the war and the inflation, deprived this definition of any basis. For in the very process in which the salaried employees grew to mass proportions, they massively forfeited what had been used to justify their privileged position: higher earnings, relative autonomy, chances of social advancement and security of employment. Their material conditions of life came to resemble those of the working class.

All the more desperate was their attempt to mark themselves off ideologically and to maintain bourgeois or corporate interpretative models as distinguishing features. 'Personality', 'Education', 'Culture', 'Profession', 'Community' – Kracauer shows how and to what end the façade of this 'house of bourgeois concepts' is continually re-erected; and at the same time he shows that the house has objectively collapsed. 'The mass of salaried employees differ from the worker proletariat in that they are spiritually homeless.' For the time being, they seek refuge in the 'shelter' provided for them by the cultural industry. A few years later the tension between proletarianized existence and bourgeois self-definition will drive them towards the National Socialists. In 1929 Kracauer could not yet know that. But the 'aura of horror' in which he sees them enshrouded already anticipates the political catastrophe that he foresaw earlier than others.[9] Not although, but because, it leads into the 'newest Germany', his study is at the same time a diagnosis of the beginning of the end of the first German republic.

It is not known what gave Kracauer the immediate impulse for his journey of discovery. Perhaps he felt provoked by Walter Ruttmann's celebrated film *Berlin, die Symphonie einer Grossstadt* (1927), whose use of montage he subjected to scathing criticism; perhaps the idea for the study came to him in the course of his analysis of the German film production of 1928, in which he first differentiated by social stratum his concept of the mass-cultural audience.[10] In retrospect, it almost seems as if he did not need a particular impulse at all. For the study of salaried employees combines themes and interests that Kracauer had been pursuing since the beginning of the 1920s. The theoretical perspectives, hermeneutic attentiveness and literary techniques that distinguish his text, however, were acquired only in a remarkable process of intellectual self-modernization.[11]

The programme of this modernization is contained *in nuce* in an essay that first appeared in 1922 in the *Frankfurter Zeitung*, under the title of 'Die Wartenden' ('Those Who Wait'). Already in this essay Kracauer is concerned with one specific social stratum's attitude towards life; and already here he formulates his findings in spatial metaphors of 'emptiness' and 'the void'. The space indicated by these metaphors is, however, not an ideological but a metaphysical one. And the stratum is not the declassed one of salaried employees, but the educated stratum to which Kracauer himself belonged, the elite of 'scholars, businessmen, doctors, lawyers, students and intellectuals of all sorts', who 'spend most of their days in the loneliness of the large cities'.[12] Finally, what forms these many individuals into a group is no sociological, but an existential condition. It is, as Kracauer explains, the 'metaphysical suffering from the lack of a higher meaning in the world' – from their 'exile from the religious sphere' – 'which makes these people companions in misfortune'.[13]

In the guise of a group-sociological diagnosis, Kracauer here expresses the sense of existence that marks the starting point of his own intellectual and literary development. In his early texts there is little trace of modernist enthusiasm, let alone of any revolutionary stance. Kracauer sees himself not at the beginning of a new age, but at the end of a historical process of 'decay' in which, with the 'disappearance of a meaning embracing reality as a whole',[14] the once saturated totality of being is broken up into isolated subjects and a chaotic multiplicity of things. Only in the perspective of a catastrophic fragmentation and de-substantialization, a breakdown of 'community bound by form'[15] and a loss of metaphysical security, is he able to perceive the modern 'thoroughly rationalized, civilized society'.[16]

Kracauer obtains the explanatory models and figures of thought which guide this perception by combining *topoi* of the contemporary conservative critique of culture with theoretical paradigms of the philosophical and sociological avant-garde. Thus his concept of a 'thoroughly rationalized, civilized society' is indebted, on the one hand, to the cultural-conservative opposition between society and community, or civilization and culture, and on the other hand, to Max Weber's disenchantment theory, which Kracauer initially appropriated with a considerable shade of cultural pessimism. His technique of translating existential and social facts into spatial images – and conversely of decoding spaces as material hieroglyphs of social facts – is inspired by Georg Simmel, under whom he studied and about whom he wrote an as yet unpublished monograph.[17] Finally, in the metaphor of 'exile from the religious sphere', it is not hard to recognize the notion of 'transcendental homelessness' which Georg Lukács introduced in his *Theory of the Novel* (1920) as a definition of modernity. Kracauer enthusiastically reviewed Lukács's book;[18] he retained its notion of 'homelessness' and revised it for the purposes of his own critique of ideology in *Die Angestellten*.

The contours of Kracauer's early diagnoses of modernity stand out more sharply in the scientific and epistemological critique of his monographs *Soziologie als Wissenschaft* (1922) and *Der Detektiv-Roman* (written between 1922 and 1925).[19] Long before Horkheimer and Adorno, he discovers that the Kantian critique of reason can be read as a kind of 'cryptography,'[20] which not only elaborates the conditions of possible knowledge, but also attests to the structure and function of modern rationality as a motor of alienation and an instrument of abstract self-assertion through domination of nature. Kracauer sees the legacy of idealistic abstraction also in contemporary 'formal sociology', which defines itself 'as an objective, value-free science' that 'strives to grasp social reality according to its necessity'.[21] In this self-definition, Kracauer counters, sociology loses its object. For in the 'empirical reality of socialized human beings'[22] no general and necessary laws prevail, nor is it possible to reduce this reality to objective facts that can be established as value-free. The world of social experience is a world of interpretations, intentional life manifestations and individual phenomena that can be known only to the extent that they are interpreted as such: i.e. as individual and meaningful.

Parallel to this epistemological critique, Kracauer's newspaper articles engage in another, increasingly pointed debate with the religious and pseudo-religious reform movements of his day. However much his own critique of contemporary civilization initially focused on metaphysical deficiencies, he was quite unable to make the *sacrificium intellectus* that joining one of those movements would have demanded. He therefore reacted with particular harshness against the 'new', intellectual '*homines religiosi*'[23] whom he encountered, for instance, in the figures of the Catholic philosopher Max Scheler[24] and the Jewish scholars Martin Buber and Franz Rosenzweig. He at first also strongly opposed the messianic philosophy of Ernst Bloch, with whom he was later to become friends.[25] Lack, as he well knew, is a bad architect and the 'home' of transcendence cannot be restored just because it might provide protection.

What alternative is left between the Scylla of abstract rationality and the Charybdis of faded doctrines of salvation? The question leads back to 'Those Who Wait'. The title of this essay is not without ironic implications. It echoes a letter from Franz Rosenzweig who had criticized Kracauer's sceptical distance from the religious reformers as 'Waiting with folded arms – and folded behind your back to boot'.[26] The attitude, however, that Kracauer proposes – he describes it as 'an attempt ... to move out of the atomized unreal world of shapeless powers and figures devoid of meaning and into the world of *reality* and the domains it encompasses'[27] – is not that of the onlooker. It may rather be associated with a figure who will reappear in another guise in *Die Angestellten*: the figure of the stranger. Kracauer carefully locates the 'one who waits' in a metaphorical context of 'exile from the religious sphere' and of 'moving into [*einkehren*] the world of reality'. For what he aims at is the stance of an intellectual who seeks to make the exile of transcendental homelessness, if not into a home, at least into a familiar dwelling. The 'one who waits' is certainly not yet the ethnologist of the 'newest Germany'. But he is already the stranger, who has decided to stay in the modern world. Because he does not know where else to go – and because he is curious.

The essay 'Those Who Wait' appeared just a few months after Kracauer had joined the editorial staff of the *feuilleton* of the *Frankfurter Zeitung* as a regular freelance contributor. The proximity of the dates indicates a connection that is not just accidental. For the intellectual modernization that Kracauer projects is also and essentially a literary one, intimately linked to the institution of the *feuilleton*. Here Kracauer found the forum that suited his interest in the quotidian and his plans for public activity. Here were literary traditions that could be used to pursue the 'big' questions not in the form of philosophical systems but in reference to the phenomena themselves. Here, finally, he was offered a field for experimentation, where the concreteness of thought he strove for could be converted into styles and genres that crossed the established boundaries between scientific disciplines as well as between journalism, literature and philosophy. Kracauer was not the only one to take advantage of the possibilities of the *feuilleton* for reflection upon, and criticism of, modernity. Authors like Joseph Roth, Ernst Bloch or Walter Benjamin likewise recognized its potential. Thanks to Kracauer's support and the prudent leadership of Benno Reifenberg, they could be engaged as regular contributors to the *Frankfurter Zeitung*.[28] Thus in this paper during the 1920s, the space 'below the line' – in other words, below the graphic marker optically separating the *feuilleton* from the other sections – became what it had never been before and would never be again: the production site of a fragmentary theory of modernity.

At first hesitantly, then from 1924 on with growing consistency and determination, Kracauer opened the *feuilleton* to the new media and genres of mass culture – photography and film, radio and popular music, sport and revue – and the distracted forms of perception and modes of reception that they engender. He analysed how the book market, with its multitude of popular genres and the hitherto scarcely noticed phenomenon of the best-seller, became transformed under the competitive pressure of these media. He studied the new codes of social communication and described the ritual of their forms and gestures. He discovered amusement palaces and hotel lobbies as centres of cult worship in which the modern age celebrates its emptiness and its distraction; and he explored the exemplary spaces of its public life: cities and streets, arcades and railway stations, restaurants and stores, and last but not least the labour exchanges and soup kitchens in which those eliminated from the economic process congregate.[29]

In these investigations Kracauer puts into practice what he resolved upon programmatically in 'Those Who Wait': he 'moves into the world of reality'. His interest, however, is not directed at reality as such, but specifically at its fugitive and imperceptible phenomena that most stubbornly resist interpretation, that fall through the mesh of theoretical systems and elude conceptual generalization. He himself coined for these phenomena the famous term 'inconspicuous surface-level expressions' [*Unscheinbare Oberflächenäusserungen*].[30] The metaphor of the surface – an updated descendant of the concepts of 'emptiness' and 'unreality' around which Kracauer's early cultural-pessimist writings revolved – is on the one hand programmatically counterposed to the 'depth' which bourgeois culture identified with genuineness, authenticity and truth. At the same time the metaphor reflects upon a basic feature of modernity itself: namely the degree to which its public sphere begins to adapt to the conditions of its technological reproducibility and to develop a 'photographic face',[31] a physiognomy modelled on the demands of the media. In *Die Angestellten* Kracauer quotes a Berlin department-store manager who describes the 'pleasant appearance' necessary for employment in his firm as a 'morally pink complexion'. Visibility here becomes the 'projection surface of a faculty of judgement that itself merely again tests suitability for superficial appearance'.[32]

Just as the metaphor of the 'morally pink complexion', precisely because of its casual nature, does not merely say what the manager thought but also betrays 'what is so self-evident to him that he does not even have to consider it',[33] so the significance that Kracauer ascribes to the surface is directly connected with its inconspicuousness. Here – according to the central thesis of his critical phenomenology – social control decreases; here, encoded as a material 'hieroglyph',[34] a social being is expressed that is masked and disguised by interested consciousness. Compared to an 'epoch's judgements about itself',[35] 'surface-level expressions' are unintentional and uncensored. When they can be successfully deciphered, the 'fundamental substance of the state of things'[36] presents itself without ideological distortion, without the 'interference of consciousness',[37] and hence 'unmediated'.[38]

Kracauer elaborated the theoretical foundations of his critical phenomenology between 1923 and 1926, in an intensive reading of Kierkegaard, Marx and a Max Weber reconsidered through the lens of Marx's early writings. In the course of this reading he translated his early, cultural-pessimist diagnosis of modernity into the context of a 'material philosophy of history'.[39] Its perspectives are formulated in his perhaps best-known essay, 'The Mass Ornament' of 1927. In the analysis of an icon of the culture of distraction – the revue performances of the Tiller Girls – Kracauer attempts in this essay to determine 'the position' which his 'epoch occupies in the historical process'.[40] In his early writings he had interpreted the history of modernity as a fall from an anterior plenitude of meaning. Now, in the 1927 essay, he conceives of it as a process of 'disenchantment', a 'demythologization' of natural bonds. In both cases, history is essentially viewed as a destructive process, a process of disintegration and desubstantialization. Accordingly, Kracauer particularly emphasizes the implications of dissolution and decomposition inherent in his new notion of 'demythologization'.[41] But whereas from the melancholy outlook of his early writings the historical process was at best acknowledged as irreversible, it is now emphatically affirmed as a necessary negation on the way to the 'breakthrough' of reason (*Vernunft*).[42] In this speculative construction modernity appears in a new light. It marks a crisis of history not because it represents the most advanced state of disenchantment – on the contrary, therein precisely lies its truth. It makes a crisis, rather, because it threatens to bring the dynamics of disenchantment to a halt. By virtue of its negative spirit of analysis, modern rationality does partake of the truth of disenchanting reason. But this progressive potential is neutralized by the increasing stabilization of capitalist relations of production. In the 'ratio' of capitalist economy, as Kracauer puts it, the 'false concreteness' of myth is reversed into its unmediated opposite, a 'false abstractness' that knows no other purpose than the 'domination and use of self-contained natural entities'.[43] This abstract rationality itself bears mythic traits, since it treats the product of its own historical destruction, i.e. capitalist productive and social relations, as if they were an immutable natural basis.

It was with good reason that Adorno assured Kracauer in 1933 that he had 'been the first of us all to tackle afresh the problems of the Enlightenment'.[44] In retrospect 'The Mass Ornament' reads like a nucleus of *The Dialectic of Enlightenment*. Unlike Horkheimer and Adorno, though, Kracauer in 1927 had not yet lost faith in the possibility of historical progress – or, more precisely, of a messianic 'breakthrough of truth', a 'reversal' of 'emptiness' into 'the fullness of being'.[45] This faith is grounded in the eschatological notion of a productive, 'revolutionizing negativity'.[46] Under its influence Kracauer in the mid-1920s commits himself to a critical strategy according to which only intensification of the destructive process of modernity offers the chance of unleashing its emancipatory and utopian energies neutralized within capitalist relations of production. Thus, when Kracauer in 'The Mass Ornament' provocatively states: 'capitalism ... rationalizes not too much, but rather *too little*',[47] he is gambling on the possibility that through further rationalization the 'spirit of capitalism' (Max Weber) will turn its inherent critical-analytical potential against itself. The process of 'demythologization' must be driven forward so that the capitalist epoch in its turn can be exposed to dissolution and 'its negativity is thought through to the end'.[48] 'America', Kracauer wrote in 1925, in an imagery familiar to his contemporaries, 'will vanish only when it fully discovers itself.'[49]

The essay 'The Mass Ornament' outlines the methodological and theoretical premises upon which Kracauer, in the second half of the 1920s, explored the cultural spaces of the anonymous public that in 1929 he would identify as the salaried class. In the beginning he saw no reason to anchor his observations in a sociological analysis of class structure. On the contrary, if Kracauer initially ascribed an emancipatory potential to capitalist culture, he did so not least because he understood this culture as a formative power capable of shaping a mass audience in which perceptual differences between classes and genders are levelled. Thus, in his 1926 essay 'Cult of Distraction', he introduces the concept of a '*homogeneous cosmopolitan audience* in which everyone has the *same* responses [*eines Sinnes ist*], from the bank director to the sales clerk, from the diva to the stenographer'.[50] The specific stratum to which the sales clerk and the stenographer belong became significant for him to the extent that he shifted the emphasis of his analyses from cinema to film, and hence from a phenomenology of the spaces and the forms of reception of mass culture to an ideological critique of its contents. A first attempt to practise film criticism as an ideological criticism of society was the essay *Film und Gesellschaft*, published in several instalments in 1927 and later reprinted in the anthology *The Mass Ornament* under the title 'The Little Shopgirls Go to the Movies'. It was followed by another serialized essay, 'Film 1928', in which Kracauer explicitly calls attention to the 'lower white-collar workers' as 'one of the principal groups of movie spectators'.[51] It is no accident that this reference occurs in a text in which Kracauer enters the lists against the 'stupidity', 'falseness' and 'meanness' of the general run of contemporary German films,[52] not just with unparalleled bitterness, but also with a confession of his own helplessness. For the more rigorously he analysed the ideology of mass media products, the more insistently the question confronted him of the kind of audience that would swallow these products. And the more insistently this question confronted him, the more urgent the need became to supplement his phenomenology and philosophy of history with sociological knowledge.

In these terms we can understand the origins of Kracauer's interest in the salaried class and the theoretical constellation from which *Die Angestellten* took its bearings. In this book, Kracauer no longer argues for an emancipatory potential, let alone a 'revolutionizing negativity', of distraction. If a few years before he had claimed that 'the homogeneous cosmopolitan audience' could become aware of its own 'reality' in the 'fragmented sequence of splendid sense impressions',[53] he now interprets mass culture as an instrument of class rule, and at the same time as the medium of a collective repression that aims to 'cast once and for all into the abyss of imageless oblivion' the ideas of 'revolution' and 'death', and therewith 'those contents that are not embraced by the construction of our social existence, but that bracket this existence itself'. Accordingly, in the need that drove the employees into the 'pleasure barracks' of the entertainment industry he is now able to discern only the symptom of a lack: the symptom of an ideological homelessness and existential despair springing from 'a life which only in a restricted sense can be called a life'. This revaluation of the concept of distraction in turn points to a comprehensive theoretical shift touching the basis of Kracauer's whole construction of modernity. It is not just the empirical research and sociological focus that fundamentally distinguish his investigation into salaried employees from his previous essays. The study is a new approach also in so far as it abandons the *grand récit* of the philosophy of history, which since the mid-1920s had underpinned his programme of deciphering unconscious surface-level expressions. As a result, Kracauer was later reproached by Adorno for lack of theoretical rigour, even for a tacit complicity with the status quo.[54] From today's viewpoint, Kracauer's sceptical detachment from speculative constructions of a general historical process appears rather as a further step in the modernization of his intellectual existence. The *grand récit* of the philosophy of history seems to be definitively invalidated. Moreover, Kracauer's abandonment of grand philosophical schemes finds its complement in a reflection upon the relation between sociological knowledge and textual representation that points forward to present-day debates in cultural theory.

'What does an ethnologist do? – he writes.'[55] Clifford Geertz's famous redefinition of ethnology as ethnography is to some extent anticipated by Kracauer. His sociological expedition into 'employee culture' is likewise a sociographical undertaking which tackles anew a question that Kracauer had already been concerned with in his early epistemological treatise *Soziologie als Wissenschaft*. It is the question of the possibility of a 'material sociology', which mediates between the claim to concreteness and the claim to valid cognition. For Kracauer, neither abstract 'idealist thought' and the scientific tradition of 'formal sociology', nor the literary genre of empirical reportage which 'generally draws from life with a leaky bucket',[56] present a satisfactory answer to this twofold claim. In the preface to his celebrated anthology *Der rasende Reporter* (1924), the writer Egon Erwin Kisch had defined the reporter as a witness without a standpoint, and reportage as a 'photography of the present'.[57] Kracauer seizes on this definition in *Die Angestellten* and turns it against the genre: in so far as reportage 'photographs life', the functional coherence of reality – its artificial, constructed quality – eludes it. This 'constructedness' demands a representational method that dissolves the fortuitous empirical coherences of the raw material, and rearranges and combines the 'observations on the basis of comprehension of their meaning'. Kracauer calls the resulting textual structure a 'mosaic'. Behind this image it is not hard to recognize the technique of another optical medium, namely the montage technique of film.

Microscopic description on the one hand, construction on the other: the representational methods that Kracauer seeks to combine are indeed so near to film close-up and montage that one could argue a posteriori from them how he visualized a good film.[58] What Kracauer conceived of as the specific materialist possibility of film – the possibility of analysing and representing reality in the medium of the optical itself, i.e. purely through focusing and cutting – he seeks in *Die Angestellten* to translate into a text. If his earlier essays deciphered surface-level phenomena as the reflex of a conceptually preformulated 'fundamental substance of an epoch', now theory forfeits its hierarchically privileged position in relation to empirical material. It infiltrates the surface, so to speak, manifesting itself in the way the tessera of the 'mosaic' are cut and in the interstices left between them.

This representational method is demonstrated in miniature in the two short texts which follow the Preface and serve as an epigraph to this book. They describe two concrete situations, rendered anonymous and general by the present tense and the indefinite articles. Each of these situations is in itself significant, but the paradoxical state of affairs they are supposed to illuminate emerges only from the mirror-image combination into which Kracauer assembles them. If one wished to define this state of affairs abstractly, one would have to speak of a contradiction between proletarianized existence and bourgeois sense of identity, and of an ideological inversion of the priority of public and seemingly private relations, reproduced for its part in the socially institutionalized separation between the sphere of work and a complementary sphere of leisure which stages the lost bourgeois status on the level of appearances. Yet this conceptual language misses precisely what matters crucially to Kracauer: the details of the situations, their complexity, the perspectives of their agents, and the tragi-comic irony inherent in them. His investigation, therefore, refrains from formulating its insight in a conceptual language removed from its material. Instead, Kracauer seeks to construct in that material. In other words, knowledge of the material's significance becomes the principle of its textual representation, so that the representation itself articulates the theory.

Under headings placed in the manner of leitmotivs the chapters of the book follow an unobtrusive narrative logic. Kracauer begins with an analysis of the selection methods that must be survived for the doors of the world of work to open at all; then he leads into the firm and its organization; and in the two succeeding sections he follows those who have been excluded from the firm and have landed up at the labour exchange or in front of the Labour Court. On the basis of this construction of material reality, the next chapters fan out across the spectrum of the ideological superstructure and its producers: from the neo-paternalism of firms and the corporate consciousness cultivated within them, via the offerings of the culture industry and the ideology of private entrepreneurs, to the collectivism of the trade unions and their cultural policy. Just as the sequence of chapters translates the central contradiction between material proletarianization and bourgeois consciousness into the structure of the text, so do the individual chapters comment upon and interpret one another reciprocally. For example, the function of the selection methods documented in the chapter entitled 'Selection' is revealed only against the background of the organization of work in the modern big firm, to which the next chapter is devoted. Similarly the chapter 'Among neighbours', which among other things exposes *divide et impera* methods within the firm, is a revealing commentary on the neo-paternalist ideologies of community described in the previous section.

The montage principle is even more obvious within the individual sections. The chapter 'Alas, so soon!', which deals with the 'laying off' of employees, begins with the description of a man who – 'Opposite the Kaiser Wilhelm Memorial Church, where the Gloriapalast and Marmor-haus salute each other like proud castles on the Dardanelles' – stationed himself with a plaque indicating that he 'was a 25-year-old unemployed salesman, who was seeking work on the open market – no matter what kind'. The plaque documents the growing unemployment that affects even people with skills. But the material does not speak for itself. For what is decisive is the fact that, as a 25-year-old, the man already counts as an older worker. The commentary appears in the advertisement quoted next, from a menswear store that would like to engage 'an older salesman of twenty-five or twenty-six'.

Like the montage of the material, the form of its linguistic mediation – quotation, conversation, report, narrative, scene, image – depends on the knowledge of its significance. The chapter 'Repair shop' reads like the outline of a story. Its narrative structure mirrors the actual connection between works council, Labour Court and labour exchange, the path of plaintiffs and complaints through the institutions. In the passages on the Labour Courts, 'close-ups' delay the progress of the bare narrative, in order to call attention to those apparent trifles which, in the light of the courtroom, 'emerge with unwonted clarity'. Individuals who have been sacked are introduced: a salesgirl who advised a friend to buy her shoes more cheaply in another store; a young employee whose private notebook was confiscated during a body-search by his firm; an elderly sales representative who seeks to furnish proof of his bourgeois origins through Latin quotations. The dramatic form of presentation is mimetically adapted to the actual situation of the hearings, through which 'nasty tricks, common practices, economic relations and social conditions are not documented . . . , but present themselves in them'.

The chapter 'A few choice specimens', inserted between the analysis of salaried employees' material living conditions and that of the ideologies superimposed on this reality, is devoted to the 'features, patterns and phenomena' which do not readily coincide with the 'image' that has been formed in the 'general consciousness' of the salaried stratum. The 'dashing' cigarette salesman who lives in a kind of 'preordained harmony' with the demands of modern life; the accountant and the cashier who turn into 'fantastical' figures from the world of E. T. A. Hoffmann during nocturnal dancing at a widows' ball; the proletarian girl 'Cricket' who has climbed to the filing department of a factory and who cannot hear any popular ditty without automatically 'chirruping along' with it; the young business employee who conducts his private correspondence on love and sexuality with methods that would be worthy of the bureaucratic organization of a large firm: Kracauer portrays these types with the love for detail of a botanist compiling a specimen-album of rare plants. What emerges, though, is no botanical system, but a small sociological archive of human figures and manifestations of life.

When *Die Angestellten* appeared in 1930, hardly a critic was able to resist the 'appeal of Kracauer's style of presentation'.[59] 'Popular descriptions of social relations', wrote the journalist Walter Dirks, 'are to Kracauer's method as amateur lyrical portrayals of landscape are to the descriptions of a good landscape morphologist'.[60] Ernst Bloch emphasized the 'sober colourfulness' of Kracauer's style,[61] Walter Benjamin its 'laconic tone', in which 'humanity' is born from the 'spirit of irony' (see p. 109). 'In Kracauer's analyses', Benjamin continues, 'there are elements of the liveliest satire that has long since withdrawn from the realm of political caricature in order to claim an epic scope corresponding to the immeasurability of its subject'. The economist Hans Speier, who shortly afterwards wrote one of the best books to date on salaried employees, placed Kracauer's description of milieux in the tradition 'of the great French and English novelists of the last century'; Kracauer not only 'measures out the space in which employees live', Speier wrote, he also renders 'the air they breathe'.[62]

That it captures the most elusive element of reality: this is a fine formula for the quality and achievement of Kracauer's prose, and at the same time one of the reasons why his text has survived and can be read anew today. A 'thick description' *avant la lettre*, Kracauer brings us 'into touch with the lives' of Berlin employees,[63] and convinces us that he 'has truly "been there"'.[64] Measured against the present state of ethnographical discussion, he undoubtedly underestimates the precariousness of his own position and the problematic nature of delimitation and distancing as means of constituting the object of his observation and description. There are relations of power and oppression, however, not just between ethnological researchers and the other culture they seek to explore, but also within this other culture's socio-political and symbolic structure. By making transparent these power structures in a skilful combination of documentation and construction, Kracauer's study transcends the ethnographical hermeneutics of 'thick description' and becomes a socio-political diagnosis pressing for reorganization and change.

## Notes

1. Siegfried Kracauer, *History. The Last Things Before the Last*, Oxford University Press, New York 1969, p. 4 (hereafter *History*).

2. Ibid., p. 4.

3. Siegfried Kracauer, *The Mass Ornament. Weimar Essays*, translated, edited and introduced by Thomas Y. Levin, Harvard University Press, Cambridge Mass. and London 1995 (hereafter *Ornament*). Kracauer compiled this collection of essays himself. Its first edition was published in 1963 by Suhrkamp Verlag, its second in 1977 with an afterword by Karsten Witte, the long-standing editor of Kracauer's selected works, *Schriften*, whose publication – also by Suhrkamp – has been under way since 1971.

4. The fact that these objections existed can be deduced not just from Reifenberg's intervention, but also from a letter from Ernst Bloch to Kracauer in October 1929, which contains the following passage: 'If the work were not able to appear in the newspaper, that would certainly be a scandal. There would be nothing left to do but swallow the pill and give the thing to *Neue Rundschau* [a celebrated journal published by S. Fischer Verlag, in which Kracauer's novel *Ginster* had appeared a year earlier].' See 'Briefwechsel Ernst Bloch–Siegfried Kracauer 1921–1966', edited and annotated by Inka Mülder-Bach, in *Ernst Bloch, Briefe 1903–1975*, edited by Karola Bloch and others, Suhrkamp Verlag, Frankfurt am Main 1985, vol. 1, p. 317. When pre-publication of *Die Angestellten* was under discussion, the *Frankfurter Zeitung* was preparing for a major staff reshuffle, coinciding with the sale of a considerable share of the newspaper publishing company to I. G. Farben and resulting politically in a marked swing to the right. Thus from 1932 on, the once decidedly liberal-democratic *Frankfurter Zeitung* championed the idea of 'taming' the Nazis by binding them into a reactionary government coalition. Kracauer's Berlin years were marked by increasing tensions with the newspaper, which gradually rid itself of its most celebrated, and politically most radical, cultural editor. Dismissal followed, a few months after Kracauer's flight from Berlin, in August 1933.

5. Letter from Benno Reifenberg to Heinrich Simon on 28 September 1929, quoted from *Marbacher Magazin 47: Siegfried Kracauer 1889–1966*, edited by Ingrid Belke and Irina Renz, Deutsche Schillergesellschaft, Marbach am Neckar 1988 (hereafter *Marbacher Magazin*), p. 51. This chronological documentation devoted to Kracauer's life and work originated as a catalogue for the exhibition organized on the occasion of its hundredth anniversary by the Deutsche Literaturarchiv in Marbach, which holds Kracauer's voluminous posthumous papers.

6. S. Kracauer, *Die Angestellten. Aus dem neuesten Deutschland*, Frankfurter Societäts-Druckerei, Abteilung Buchverlag, Frankfurt am Main 1930. The first post-war German edition of the text appeared in 1959. It was published by the Verlag für Demoskopie, Allensbach and Bonn, as the first volume in the series *Klassiker der Umfrageforschung* [Classics of Public-Opinion Research]. The grotesque misunderstanding that led to this classification is a small but telling indication of the intellectual decline affecting German social sciences as a result of the huge emigration after 1933. In the context of the edition of Kracauer's collected writings, the text was republished in *Schriften*, vol. 1, edited by Karsten Witte, Suhrkamp Verlag, Frankfurt am Main 1971, pp. 205–304.

The steadily growing literature on Kracauer in recent years contains comparatively few items relating to *Die Angestellten*. One exception in the English-speaking world is

David Frisby, *Fragments of Modernity: Theories of Modernity in the Work of Simmel, Kracauer and Benjamin*, Polity Press, Cambridge 1985, pp. 158–73. German-language titles include: Inka Mülder-Bach, *Siegfried Kracauer – Grenzgänger zwischen Theorie und Literatur. Seine frühen Schriften 1913–1933*, Metzler, Stuttgart 1985, pp. 115–25; Rolf Lindner, *Die Entdeckung der Stadtkultur. Soziologie aus der Erfahrung der Reportage*, Suhrkamp Verlag, Frankfurt am Main 1990; Henri Band, 'Massenkultur versus Angestelltenkultur. Siegfried Kracauers Auseinandersetzung mit Phänomenen der modernen Kultur in der Weimarer Republik', in Norbert Krenzlin, ed., *Zwischen Angstmetapher und Terminus. Theorien der Massenkultur seit Nietzsche*, Akademie Verlag, Berlin 1992, pp. 73–101; Henri Band, 'Siegfried Kracauers Expedition in die Alltagswelt der Berliner Angestellten', in Andreas Volk, ed., *Siegfried Kracauer. Zum Werk des Feuilletonisten, Filmwissenschaftlers und Soziologen (Soziographie*, vol. 7 [1994], no. 1/2), Zurich 1996, pp. 213–31.

7. 'The "reporter" deals in sensation – that is implicit in the foreign term we use for journalists operating at an American pace', wrote Egon Erwin Kisch in the preface to his classic anthology of reportage first published in 1924. See Egon Erwin Kisch, *Der rasende Reporter*, Kiepenheuer und Witsch, Cologne 1985, p. 7.

8. On the history of salaried employees in Germany, see Jürgen Kocka, *Die Angestellten in der deutschen Geschichte. 1850–1890*, Vandenhoeck und Ruprecht, Göttingen 1981; Jürgen Kocka, 'White Collar Workers and Industrial Society in Imperial Germany', in George Iggers, ed., *The Social History of Politics. Critical Perspectives in West German Historical Writing Since 1945*, Berg Publishers, Leamington Spa, Dover and Heidelberg 1985, pp. 113–36. For a comparative treatment, see Werner Mangold, 'Angestelltengeschichte und Angestelltensoziologie in Deutschland, England und Frankreich', in Jürgen Kocka, ed., *Angestellte im europäischen Vergleich. Die Herausbildung angestellter Mittelschichten seit dem späten 19. Jahrhundert*, Vandenhoeck und Ruprecht, Göttingen 1981, pp. 11–38. In accordance with the specific political importance of the stratum, a sociology of employees developed earlier in Germany than in other countries. One pioneering study was Emil Lederer's *Die Privatangestellten in der modernen Wirtschaftsentwicklung*, Tübingen 1912. With Jakob Marshak, Lederer was also responsible for the summary 'Der neue Mittelstand', in *Grundriss der Sozialökonomik*, vol. 9, part 1, Tübingen 1926, pp. 120–41, to which Kracauer was indebted for crucial particulars of his own investigation. Shortly after his study, a number of other trailblazing works were written on the topic, some of which were published in Germany only after the Second World War. See Theodor Geiger, *Die soziale Schichtung des deutschen Volkes*, Stuttgart 1932, reprinted Stuttgart 1967 and Darmstadt 1972; Erich Fromm, *Arbeiter und Angestellte am Vorabend des Dritten Reichs. Eine sozialpsychologische Untersuchung*, edited by Wolfgang Bonss, Deutsche Verlagsanstalt, Stuttgart 1980 (the original English manuscript of this study, 'German Workers 1929 – A Survey, its Methods and Results', was written in 1929/30); Hans Speier, *Die Angestellten vor dem Nationalsozialismus. Ein Beitrag zum Verständnis der deutschen Sozialstruktur 1918–1933*, Göttingen 1977, reprinted Fischer Verlag, Frankfurt am Main 1989 (Speier's book is the revised version of a study completed in 1933, which for political reasons could not be published at the time).

9. In August 1930, Kracauer wrote in a letter to Adorno: 'The situation in Germany is more than serious. . . . We are going to have three or four million unemployed and I can see no way out. A disaster is hanging over this country and I am convinced that it is not just capitalism. That capitalism may become bestial is not due to the economy alone. (How am I to formulate the causes? I simply keep noticing in France, even though there's plenty to criticize there, all the things that have been destroyed here: basic decency, good nature in general, and with it people's trust in one another.)' Quoted from *Marbacher Magazin*, pp. 58 and 63. In his Berlin years Kracauer deliberately attempted by journalistic means to prevent the spread of fascism in the 'middle strata'. See on this, apart from the essay 'Revolt of the Middle

Classes. An Examination of the Tat Circle' (1931), in *Ornament*, pp. 107–27, the texts 'Zwischen Blut und Geist', in *Schriften*, vol. 5, ed. Inka Mülder-Bach, Suhrkamp Verlag, Frankfurt am Main 1990 (hereafter *Schriften* 5, with part number), 3: *Aufsätze 1932–1965*, pp. 93–6; 'Gestaltschau oder Politik?' (1932), in *Schriften* 5, 3, pp. 118–24; 'Wunschträume der Gebildeten' (1932), in *Schriften* 5, 3, pp. 154–9; and 'Theologie gegen Nationalismus' (1933), in *Schriften* 5, 3, pp. 186–90. Kracauer's contributions to the pioneering series 'Wie erklären sich grosse Bucherfolge?' ['How can best-sellers be explained?'] also belong in the context of this argument. See: 'Richard Voss, *Zwei Menschen*' (1931), in *Schriften* 5, 2: *Aufsätze 1927–1932*, pp. 287–94; and 'Bemerkungen zu Frank Thiess' (1931), in *Schriften* 5, 2, pp. 312–18. The essay 'On Bestsellers and their Audience' (1931), in *Ornament*, pp. 89–98, is a synopsis of the methods and results of this series.

10. See 'Film 1928' in *Ornament*, pp. 307–20. This essay, which first appeared in *Frankfurter Zeitung* in November and December 1928 under the title 'Der heutige Film und sein Publikum', also contains the critique of Ruttmann that Kracauer took up again and formulated in greater detail in his history of Weimar cinema *From Caligari to Hitler* (1947).

11. For Kracauer's Weimar period writings, see Mülder-Bach, *Siegfried Kracauer: Grenzgänger zwischen Theorie und Literatur*, Mülder-Bach, 'Nachwort', in *Schriften* 5, 3, pp. 360–84; Frisby, *Fragments of Modernity*, pp. 109–86; Levin, 'Introduction', in *Ornament*, pp. 1–30; Gertrud Koch, K*racauer: Zur Einführung*, Junius Verlag, Hamburg 1996.

12. *Ornament*, p. 129.

13. Ibid., pp. 129ff.

14. *Schriften* 5, 1: *Aufsätze 1915–26*, p. 117 ('Georg von Lukács' Romantheorie', 1921).

15. *Ornament*, p. 132.

16. *Schriften 1*, p. 105.

17. 'Georg Simmel. Ein Beitrag zur Deutung des geistigen Lebens unserer Zeit', undated typescript (*c.* 1919/20), Kracauer-Nachlass, Deutsches Literaturarchiv, Marbach am Neckar. Only one chapter of this study has been published to date; it first appeared in 1920, under the title 'Georg Simmel', in the journal *Logos*, and was reprinted in *Ornament*, pp. 225–57. For the imagery of space in Simmel and Kracauer, see Anthony Vidler, 'Agoraphobia. Spatial Estrangement in Simmel and Kracauer', in *New German Critique* 54, Fall 1991, special issue on Siegfried Kracauer, pp. 31–45.

18. See note 14 above.

19. *Soziologie als Wissenschaft* was republished in Kracauer, *Schriften* 1, pp. 7–101. The study on the detective novel, of which only the chapter 'The Hotel Lobby' (included in *Ornament*, pp. 173–85) appeared during Kracauer's lifetime, was first published fully in *Schriften* 1, pp. 103–204.

20. Theodor W. Adorno, 'Der wunderliche Realist' (1964), in *Noten zur Literatur*, vol. 3, Suhrkamp Verlag, Frankfurt am Main 1965, p. 84. Adorno's highly problematic portrait of his friend and teacher has recently been translated into English: *Notes on Literature*, vol. 2, translated by Shierry Weber Nicholsen, Columbia University Press, New York 1992, pp. 58–75. For the Kracauer–Adorno relationship, see Martin Jay, 'Adorno and Kracauer: Notes on a Troubled Friendship' (1978), in his *Permanent Exiles. Essays in the Intellectual Migration from Germany to America*, Columbia University Press, New York 1986, pp. 217–36.

21. Kracauer, 'Soziologie als Wissenschaft', in *Schriften* 1, p. 9.

22. Ibid., p. 62.

23. Letter to Leo Löwenthal, 16 December 1921, quoted from *Marbacher Magazin*, p. 36.

24. For Kracauer's early critique of Scheler, see especially the essay 'Catholicism and Relativism' (1921), *Ornament*, pp. 203–11. For his debate with Buber and

Rosenzweig, see the review of Buber's *Ich und Du* (1922) published under the title 'Martin Buber' (1923) and included in *Schriften* 5, 1, pp. 236–42; also the celebrated essay 'The Bible in German' (1926), *Ornament*, pp. 189–201, a critical analysis of the first volumes of Buber and Rosenzweig's translation of the Bible.

25. See the essay 'Prophetentum' (1922), in *Schriften* 5, 1, pp. 196–204, a withering critique of Bloch's *Thomas Münzer als Theologe der Revolution* (1921). Kracauer's critique of Buber's and Rosenzweig's translation of the Bible prepared the ground for his reconciliation with Bloch. Their friendship, which though not free of conflict was close and survived exile, is documented by the 'Briefwechsel' cited in note 4 above.

26. Letter to Kracauer, 12 December 1921, quoted from *Marbacher Magazin*, p. 36.

27. *Ornament*, p. 139.

28. On the *feuilleton* section of the *Frankfurter Zeitung* in the 1920s, see Almut Todorov, *Das Feuilleton der Frankfurter Zeitung während der Weimarer Republik: zur Rhetorik einer publizistischen Institution*, Max Niemeyer Verlag, Tübingen 1995.

29. Kracauer's essays are catalogued in Thomas Y. Levin, *Siegfried Kracauer. Eine Bibliographie seiner Schriften*, Deutsche Schillergesellschaft, Marbach am Neckar 1989. For the period 1921–33, i.e. the years with the *Frankfurter Zeitung*, the bibliography lists almost 2,000 titles. Kracauer himself put together two selections of these essays: *Ornament*, and the anthology of short prose texts *Strassen in Berlin und anderswo*, Suhrkamp Verlag, Frankfurt am Main 1964. Both were incorporated in the expanded selection of essays comprising the three-part volume 5 of his *Schriften*, published in 1990. This volume does not include the film essays, which will be published in *Schriften* 6. A selection of texts on film appeared in Kracauer, *Kino. Essays, Studien, Glossen zum Film*, edited by Karsten Witte, Suhrkamp Verlag, Frankfurt am Main 1974, and also in Kracauer, *Schriften* 2: *Von Caligari zu Hitler*, edited by Karsten Witte, Suhrkamp Verlag, Frankfurt am Main 1979, Appendix 1: 'Filmkritiken 1924–1939'. The recently published volume *Berliner Nebeneinander. Ausgewählte Feuilletons 1930–33*, edited by Andreas Volk, Edition Epoca, Zurich 1996, contains texts from Kracauer's Berlin period not included in *Schriften* 5.

30. *Ornament*, p. 75 ('The Mass Ornament', 1927).

31. *Ornament*, p. 59 ('Photography', 1927).

32. Gertrud Koch, *Kracauer: Zur Einführung* (see note 11 above), p. 55.

33. *Schriften* 5, 2, p. 188 ('Über Arbeitsnachweise', 1930).

34. Ibid., p. 186.

35. *Ornament*, p. 75 ('The Mass Ornament', 1927).

36. Ibid.

37. *Schriften* 5, 2, p. 186.

38. *Ornament*, p. 75.

39. Kracauer employs this concept in a letter to Bloch on 27 May 1926: Bloch, *Briefe*, vol. 1, p. 274.

40. *Ornament*, p. 75. For a more detailed analysis of the essay, see Inka Mülder-Bach, 'Der Umschlag der Negativität. Zur Verschränkung von Phänomenologie, Geschichtsphilosophie und Filmästhetik in Kracauers Metaphorik der "Oberfläche"', in *Deutsche Vierteljahrsschrift für Literaturwissenschaft und Geistesgeschichte*, 61, 1987, pp. 359–73; Mülder-Bach, 'Nachwort', in *Schriften* 5, 3, pp. 369ff. For an English paraphrase of this analysis, see Levin, 'Introduction', in *Ornament*, pp. 66ff.

41. *Ornament*, p. 80.

42. Ibid.

43. Ibid., pp. 80ff.

44. Letter to Kracauer, 12 January 1933 (Kracauer-Nachlass, Deutsches Literaturarchiv, Marbach am Neckar).

45. *Schriften* 5, 1, p. 371 ('Die Denkfläche', 1926).

46. *Schriften* 5, 2, p. 166 ('Zwei Arten der Mitteilung', c. 1929). On this concept, see Mülder-Bach, 'Der Umschlag der Negativität' (see note 40 above); on Kracauer's

secularized messianism, see also Miriam Hansen, 'Decentric Perspectives: Kracauer's Early Writings on Film and Mass Culture', *New German Critique*, 54, Fall 1991, pp. 47–76.

47. *Ornament*, p. 81.

48. Ibid., p. 73 ('Die Reise und der Tanz', 1925).

49. *Schriften* 5, 1, p. 305 ('Der Künstler in dieser Zeit', 1925).

50. *Ornament*, p. 325. On Kracauer's concept of 'audience', see Heide Schlüpmann, 'Phenomenology of Film. On Siegfried Kracauer's Writings of the 1920s', *New German Critique*, 40, Winter 1987, pp. 97–114; Heide Schüpmann, 'Der Gang ins Kino – ein Ausgang aus selbstverschuldeter Unmündigkeit. Zum Begriff des Publikums in Kracauers Essayistik der Zwanziger Jahre', in Michael Kessler and Thomas Y. Levin, eds, *Siegfried Kracauer. Neue Interpretationen*, Stauffenberg Verlag, Tübingen 1990, pp. 267–84.

51. *Ornament*, p. 318.

52. Ibid., p. 307.

53. Ibid., p. 326.

54. Adorno, 'Der wunderliche Realist', pp. 90ff.

55. Clifford Geertz, *The Interpretation of Cultures*, Basic Books, New York 1977, p. 19.

56. *Schriften* 5, 2, p. 186 ('Über Arbeitsnachweise', 1930). Kracauer followed the contemporary literature of reportage carefully and commented on it in a number of essays. See, for instance, 'Ein Buch von der Ruhr' (1931), *Schriften* 5, 2, pp. 393–5; 'Der operierende Schriftsteller' (1932), *Schriften* 5, 3, pp. 26–30; 'Zu einem Roman aus der Konfektion. Nebst einem Exkurs über die soziale Romanreportage' (1932), *Schriften* 5, 3, pp. 75–9; 'Grossstadtjugend ohne Arbeit' (1932), *Schriften* 5, 3, pp. 124–7.

57. Kisch, *Der rasende Reporter*, pp. 7ff.

58. See Michael Schröter, 'Weltzerfall und Rekonstruktion. Zur Physiognomik Siegfried Kracauers', in *Text + Kritik*, no. 68: *Siegfried Kracauer*, Edition Text + Kritik, Munich 1980, p. 33.

59. Ernst W. Eschmann, 'Die Angestellten. Ergänzungen zu S. Kracauer', in *Die Tat* 22 (1930), vol. 2, p. 460. As the place of publication suggests – *Die Tat* was a central organ of the 'Conservative Revolution' – in political terms Eschmann was one of Kracauer's sharpest critics. For Kracauer's analysis of the *Tat* circle, see note 9 above.

60. Walter Dirks, 'Zur Situation der deutschen Angestellten. Aus Anlass eines Buches', in *Die Schildgenossen*, 11 (1931), p. 248.

61. Ernst Bloch, 'Künstliche Mitte' (1929), in his *Erbschaft dieser Zeit*, Verlag Oprecht & Helbing, Zurich 1935, reprinted Suhrkamp Verlag, Frankfurt am Main 1977, p. 33.

62. Hans Speier, 'Die Angestellten', in *Magazin der Wirtschaft*, 6, 1930, p. 602. For Speier's book on employees, see note 8 above.

63. Clifford Geertz, *The Interpretation of Cultures*, p. 16.

64. Clifford Geertz, *Works and Lives. The Anthropologist as Author*, Stanford University Press, Stanford 1988, pp. 4–5.

# The Salaried Masses

Siegfried Kracauer

*Translated by Quintin Hoare*

For Benno Reifenberg
as a tribute to our close friendship
and our collaboration

# Preface

No question about it, industry and commerce find themselves in a particularly difficult situation today. And the purpose of the present work is to help remedy this, though it deals less with the needs of employers than with those of salaried staff. The former have been better known than the latter hitherto, after all, and the elucidation of social and human shortcomings always in the long run redounds to the advantage of the collectivity.

The illustrative material for the work has been collected in Berlin, since it is there rather than in any other German city or region that the condition of the salariat presents itself in the most extreme form. Only from its extremes can reality be revealed.

Reference has been made mainly to large-scale enterprises. Conditions in many small and medium enterprises, of course, are of a different nature. But the big firm is the model of the future. Moreover, the problems it poses and the needs common to its mass of employees increasingly determine our domestic political life and thought.

The core of the work is made up of direct quotations, conversations and observations. These should be seen not as examples of any theory, but as exemplary instances of reality.

The work is a diagnosis and, as such, deliberately refrains from putting forward proposals for improvements. Prescriptions are not appropriate everywhere and least of all here, where the primary aim was to become fully aware of a situation still barely explored. Knowledge of this situation, moreover, is not just the necessary precondition for every change, but actually itself encompasses a change: for once the situation in question is thoroughly known, it must be acted upon on the basis of this new awareness. In any case, the reader will have no trouble finding in the work a whole number of remarks transcending the analysis.

On the occasion of the work's pre-publication in the *feuilleton* section of the *Frankfurter Zeitung* (minor changes apart, the book edition is identical to the newspaper version), I received a whole range of letters testifying to the widespread interest in the question treated here. Coming chiefly from prominent men of affairs, from university teachers, from sociologists and from employees themselves, the majority of them express satisfaction at the very existence of such a work. Of the critical comments, some are based on misunderstandings. Thus I have been taxed, for example, with maintaining that even such functions as machines cannot handle could be coped with today by people scarcely able to read or write; whereas, on the contrary, I have expressly taken into account the necessity of a good education for senior staff. People likewise dispute numerous effects of rationalization that I am not alone in considering indisputable; or seek to deny the widely encountered economy of patronage, whose existence it is part of my task to indicate. At all events, part of the real point of an undertaking such as this is to provoke public discussion.

In conclusion, I thank all those who have supported me. Numerous employers, personnel managers of large firms, deputies, works-council members and representatives of the various employee unions have assisted in the realization of my work, by willingly furnishing me opportunities for discussion. Nor should I on any account fail to mention my many conversations with employees themselves: I should like this little book truly to speak of them, since they cannot easily speak for themselves.

*S. Kracauer*
*January 1930*

## I

*Before a Labour Court, a dismissed female employee is suing for either restoration of her job or compensation. Her former boss, a male department manager, is there to represent the defending firm. Justifying the dismissal, he explains* inter alia*: 'She didn't want to be treated like an employee, but like a lady.' In private life, the department manager is six years younger than the employee.*

## II

*One evening an elegant gentleman, doubtless a person of some standing in the clothes trade, enters the lobby of a big-city night club in the company of his girlfriend. It is obvious at first glance that the girlfriend's side-line is to stand behind a counter for eight hours. The cloakroom lady addresses the girlfriend: 'Perhaps Madam would like to leave her coat?'*

# Unknown territory

'But you can already find all that in novels', one private employee replied, when I asked her to tell me something about her life in the office. I got to know her one Sunday on the train journey to a Berlin suburb. She was returning from a wedding banquet that had lasted the whole day and, as she herself admitted, she was a bit tipsy. Without prompting she divulged her boss, who was a soap manufacturer; she had already been working for three years as his private secretary. He was a bachelor and admired her lovely dark eyes.

'Your eyes really are very lovely', I said.

'We go out every evening. Sometimes he takes me to the café with him in the afternoon too, and then we don't go back again. Do you see my shoes? I wear my shoes out every few months, dancing. What's your interest in the office anyway? I really don't talk to the office staff – those girls are green with envy.'

'Will you be marrying your boss one day?'

'Whatever gave you that idea? Wealth doesn't attract me. I'm sticking to my fiancé.'

'Does your fiancé know . . .'

'I'm not such a fool. What I've got going with my boss is no one else's business.'

It turned out that her fiancé was currently managing the Seville branch of a lingerie firm. I advised her to visit him. 'There's the world exhibition on now in Barcelona . . .'

'You can't just walk across the sea', she retorted.

Despite my earnest assurances, she would not believe that Spain could be reached overland. Later on she means to run a little inn with her intended, somewhere not far from Berlin. They will have a garden and in summer people will come from far and wide . . .

You cannot, as the secretary thinks, find it all in novels. On the contrary, information about her and her kind is hard to obtain.

Hundreds of thousands of salaried employees throng the streets of Berlin daily, yet their life is more unknown than that of the primitive tribes at whose habits those same employees marvel in films. The officials of employee unions, as is to be expected, only rarely look beyond the particular to the construction of society. Employers are generally not impartial witnesses. Intellectuals are either employees themselves or, if independent, usually find employees too commonplace to interest them. Even radical intellectuals do not easily get behind the exoticism of a commonplace existence. And how about the employees themselves? They are least conscious of their situation. But surely their existence is spent in full public view? It is precisely its public nature that protects it from discovery, just like the 'Letter to Her Majesty' in Edgar Allan Poe's tale: nobody notices the letter because it is out on display. Powerful forces are admittedly in play, anxious to prevent anyone noticing anything here.

So it is high time the light of publicity fell on the public condition of salaried employees, whose situation has been utterly transformed since the pre-war years.

In simple numerical terms: there are 3.5 million salaried employees in Germany today, of whom 1.2 million are women. Over a period in which the number of workers has not yet doubled, salary-earners have multiplied almost five times. Nowadays there is a salaried employee for every fifth worker. Civil servants likewise have experienced a sharp increase.

Almost half this huge mass of salaried employees work in commerce, banking and transport. It is noteworthy that over recent years salaried staff in industry have increased particularly fast, so that they already number 1.35 million. The remaining half million are accounted for by public authorities, organizations, etc.

So far as their occupational classification is concerned, by far the most important group is that of commercial employees, who number 2.25 million. These are followed at a considerable distance by the remaining groups (of almost equal size) comprising office, technical and supervisory staff – who in each case number about a quarter of a million.

The causes of the vast increase may be sought in the specialist literature. They are bound up basically with structural changes in the economy: development towards the modern large-scale enterprise, with a simultaneous transformation of its organizational form; growth of the apparatus of distribution; expansion of social security and large associations regulating the collective life of numerous groups – all this has driven the figures upwards, despite every retrenchment. The fact that precisely so many women have flooded into salaried jobs can be explained, in particular, by the rise in the surplus of women, by the economic consequences of war and inflation, and by the need of the new generation of women for economic independence. The dialectical transformation of quantity into quality has not failed to occur – or, rather, quality has been transformed into quantity.

The change has been caused by the oft-mentioned rationalization. Ever since capitalism has existed, of course, within its defined boundaries rationalization has always occurred. Yet the rationalization period from 1925 to 1928 represents a particularly important chapter, which has produced the irruption of the machine and 'assembly-line' methods into the clerical departments of big firms. Thanks to this reorganization carried out on the American pattern – and which is still far from complete – large sections of the new salaried masses have a lesser function in the labour process than they had before. There are a great many unskilled and semi-skilled employees today performing mechanical tasks. (For instance, in the one-price stores that have sprung up recently, salesgirls' duties are mechanized.) The former 'NCOs of capital' have become an imposing army whose ranks contain a growing number of mutually interchangeable private soldiers.

No less a person than Emil Lederer calls it 'an objective fact, if one maintains that salaried employees share the fate of the proletariat'. He even hazards the assertion that 'today ... the social space in which we still find modern slavery ... is no longer the plant in which the great mass of workers work; that social space is instead the office.'[1] There is room for argument about his apportionment of slavery, but the proletarianization of employees is beyond dispute. At all events, similar social conditions prevail for broad layers of salary-earners as for the proletariat itself. An industrial reserve army of salaried employees has come into being. The view that this is a temporary phenomenon is countered by the alternative view that it could be dismantled only along with the system that has conjured it up – a discussion about which we shall have more to say. The existential insecurity of salaried staff has increased, moreover, and their prospect of independence has almost entirely disappeared. In view of this, can the belief be sustained that they constitute some kind of a 'new middle class'? We shall see that illusions produced for salary-earners encounter a sizeable demand.

At least, the realism of salaried employees has been intensified by their straitened material circumstances. Average earnings that for the semi-skilled begin at less than 150 Marks, and that for more experienced

1. 'Die Umschichtung des Proletariats' ['The restructuring of the proletariat'], included in the volume *Angestellte und Arbeiter* ['Salaried employee and worker'] published by the Afa-Bund, Freier Volksverlag, Berlin 1928.

staff in senior positions barely reach 500 Marks, make them feel like workers at least in the economic respect. And the income of female employees is normally 10 or 15 per cent lower. In the struggle for better working conditions, some 30 per cent of salaried employees have organized themselves in unions. The three main associations are:

- the Allgemeine Freie Angestelltenbund (Afa-Bund), with over 400,000 members. Affiliated to this are the Zentralverband der Angestellten (ZdA), the Deutsche Werkmeisterverband, the Bund der technischen Angestellten und Beamten (Butab), and the Allgemeine Verband der Deutschen Bankangestellten – plus seamen's associations and almost all artists' unions. An organizational agreement governs the Free Afa-Bund's relations with the Allgemeine Deutsche Gewerkschaftsbund [Confederation of German Trade Unions], while politically it is attached to the Social-Democratic Party. It campaigns for the extension of socio-political legislation and for transforming the capitalist system into a socialized economy.
- the Gewerkschaftsbund der Angestellten (GdA). This is a unitary association encompassing salaried staff from all trades, mainly commercial and office employees. Together with the Deutsche Bankbeamtenverein and the Allgemeine Verband der Versicherungsangestellten – with which it is organized in the Deutsche Gewerkschaftsring (incorporating the Hirsch-Dunckersche Gewerkverein) – it forms the 376,000-member-strong 'liberal-national' group in the employees' movement. Its stance is basically democratic. In terms of union politics, it by and large agrees with the Afa-Bund.
- the Gesamtverband Deutscher Angestelltengewerkschaften (Gedag), with over 400,000 members. Its principal associations are the Deutschnationale Handlungsgehilfen-Verband (DHV) and the Verband der weiblichen Handels- und Büroangestellten. The Gedag belongs to the Christian-national wing of the union movement. It is an opponent of socialism and tainted with anti-semitism. Any common denominator between its often radical union conduct in wage negotiations and its bourgeois-corporatist ideology is hard to find.

In addition, there is also a Reichsbund Deutscher Angestellten-Berufsverbände (with 60,000 members), which is affiliated to the Reichsausschuss werksgemeinschaftlicher Verbände. It is perhaps worth mentioning that the Vereinigung der leitenden Angestellten (Vela) refrains from trade-union activity, contenting itself with sickness relief, a burial fund and general representation.

Those are a few facts. They roughly outline the territory into which this little expedition – perhaps more of an adventure than any film trip to Africa – is to journey. For as it seeks out employees, it leads at the same time to the heart of the modern big city. Sombart once observed that our big German cities today are not industrial cities, but cities of salaried employees and civil servants. If that holds true for any city, it does for Berlin. Here, the economic process engendering salaried employees en masse has advanced furthest; here, the decisive practical and ideological clashes take place; here, the form of public life determined by the needs of employees – and by people who for their part would like to determine those needs – is particularly striking. Berlin today is a city with a pronounced employee culture: i.e. a culture made by employees for employees and seen by most employees as a culture. Only in Berlin, where links to roots and the soil are so reduced that weekend outings can become the height of fashion, may the reality of salaried employees be grasped. It also comprises a good part of Berlin's reality.

Does this reality submit to normal reportage? For a number of years now, reportage has enjoyed in Germany the highest favour among all types of representation, since it alone is said to be able to capture life unposed. Writers scarcely know any higher ambition than to report; the reproduction of observed reality is the order of the day. A hunger for directness that is undoubtedly a consequence of the malnutrition caused by German idealism. Reportage, as the self-declaration of concrete existence, is counterposed to the abstractness of idealist thought, incapable of approaching reality through any mediation. But existence is not captured by being at best duplicated in reportage. The latter has been a legitimate counterblow against idealism, nothing more. For it merely loses its way in the life that idealism cannot find, which is equally unapproachable for both of them. A hundred reports from a factory do not add up to the reality of the factory, but remain for all eternity a hundred views of the factory. Reality is a construction. Certainly life must be observed for it to appear. Yet it is by no means contained in the more or less random observational results of reportage; rather, it is to be found solely in the mosaic that is assembled from single observations on the basis of comprehension of their meaning. Reportage photographs life; such a mosaic would be its image.

# Selection

'Why do you want to be a commercial employee?' 'Because I like that sort of job.' 'Which line of business?' 'Soft furnishings.' 'Why precisely that?' 'Because I find the work light and clean.'

Another answer to the first question: 'Because I prefer a job that's not manual.'

Another answer again: 'I'd like to be in sales.' 'Why don't you go for a craft?' 'I wouldn't like to work in a factory.'

With answers like this, boys and girls leaving school fill out question-naires obtained from the career guidance department of the Zentralver-band der Angestellten. The spelling is not always flawless, and the unruly grammar of colloquial speech often overlays the learned rules of written German. A year or two later and apprentices with their literary spurs will write confidently in their business letters: 'Most respectfully yours . . .'.

A non-manual job, preferably in sales, work that's light and clean – the rosy dreams do not all come to fruition. At any rate, it is not enough to feel the call, you must also be chosen – chosen by the authorities driving forward the economic process that drives them.

In Dresden, shoemakers are said to have decided recently to employ only apprentices who have completed two years of second-ary school. So a person may not even patch and sole just from an inner inclination. Such folly shows how ingrained the certification system is in our nature, as was observed with some resignation at the last trade-union congress. And if not in our nature, then still in the basis of our contemporary social system. We all know (or prob-ably do not know) the various certificates whose magic influence alone opens certain spheres in the civil-service hierarchy. An advanced certificate is sought nowadays as a qualification for upper-middle civil servants – a requirement that Severing has fortunately opposed.[2] Who, after the demise of the old class state, would not have predicted the same fate for these chinoiseries as for the ornaments on the Kurfürstendamm? Meanwhile, they flourish in the private sector too – and not just as arabesques. Big banks and many other commercial and industrial concerns restrict entry into the bliss of their clerical departments to young people with a certificate of secondary education, and they prefer those who have the advanced level. In Berlin, according to reliable information, out of a hundred commercial trainees, fifty might have gone on to complete the final year of secondary education. Of the fortunate certificate-holders, many remain confined throughout their lives to an activity that every ambitious former elementary-school pupil could perform just as well; a higher level of education by no means always ensures a higher salary; retrenchment measures, and other evils termed strokes of fate, hit qualified and unqualified alike. But since the powers-that-be view qualification certificates as talismans, everyone materially able to do so chases after them and seeks to enhance his own monopoly value as much as possible. The rush for further education surpasses the desire for knowledge, and technical employees turned out by vocational schools are now establishing graduate associations. Before long everyone will have a certificate for something. One member of the Deutsche Bankbeamtenverein, who in conversation with me could not hide his satisfaction at the thought that all bank employees were qualified, made the following comment with direct reference to this circumstance: 'Some of them come from good middle-class families. Their level is definitely not proletarian.' The comment is instructive in two respects. It expresses not merely an important aim of the qualification system, but also the fact that this aim is being achieved. If certain certificates may really be necessary, while others are to be explained by the shortage of lebensraum, the fact is that most people with either certificate of secondary schooling are of medium- or petit-bourgeois origin. Proletarian children must be very gifted to push beyond the eight years of elementary school, and once they have climbed sufficiently high, they often disappear from view like Indian fakirs. And since society mainly gives privileges to members of the middle class, who know from birth what is right, it creates for itself a kind of bodyguard in the enterprise. This is all the more reliable when it gets its hands on handsome weapons in the form of certificates and diplomas, with which it can cut a dash and grow rich. That bank

2. Carl Severing, former trade-union leader who served as SPD minister of the interior in the late 1920s.

The *Abitur* is a leaving examination at the end of grammar or senior-high schooling, i.e. after thirteen years' education, roughly equivalent to British A-levels. The *Einjährige* was a 'middle' certificate after ten years, roughly equivalent to GCSE.

clerk was truly singing his colleagues' praises when he said that their level was definitely not proletarian. The guard may die, but it does not surrender to an outlawed attitude: so the system protects itself against disintegration.

Other examples will be presented to show how aware salaried employees are of their status. And if the associations combined in the Afa-Bund strive for the certification system to be abolished, that is merely a logical consequence of socialist trains of thought.


'Let everyone be employed at the job he is best capable of performing – according to his abilities, his knowledge, his psychological and physical qualities: according, in short, to the specific character of his whole personality. The right person in the right place!' These phrases come originally from an O. and Partners management announcement at the end of 1927, and were intended to prepare the company's salaried staff for aptitude tests then being planned. Whole personality, right person and right place: the words drawn from the dictionary of a defunct idealist philosophy give the impression that what is involved in the test procedures currently being implemented is a genuine selection of persons. Neither in O. and Partners nor in other firms, however, do the majority of employees carry out activities requiring a personality, let alone 'the specific character of a personality'. And forget about the 'right person'! Jobs are precisely not vocations tailored to so-called personalities, but jobs in the enterprise, created according to the needs of the production and distribution process. Only in the upper layers of the social hierarchy does the true personality begin: this, however, is no longer subject to the pressure of testing. So aptitude tests may at best determine whether employees are particularly adept at specific jobs. Telephone girl or shorthand typist – that is the question. A clarification not without importance, since it means that such tests performed in the enterprise help its own interests more than they help the right person. A passage in the management announcement, intended to make any change in type of employment dependent upon test results, likewise speaks of this: 'An upwards or downwards alteration of pay occurs only if the employee in question receives a better or less good job.' The luck of personality, then, possibly does not count for much.

The same economic logic that ever more rationally moulds the enterprise also undoubtedly engenders the attempt fully to rationalize the former inchoate human mass. As its champion (albeit not wholly qualified in socio-political terms), Professor William Stern recently gave his views on the subject of tests for employees at an enlarged Afa conference. He heads the Hamburg Society for Advocates of Applied Psychology, which has been involved in the O. and Partners tests.

The conclusion to be drawn from his explanations is that a commercial employee is something infinitely more complicated than a worker. Where a simple functional test is normally sufficient for the latter, the greater demands imposed by commercial occupations mean that the former can be fathomed only by a 'total view' – even if only qualities relevant to his work are to be crystallized out. They experiment with him: accounting tests, telephone tests, etc. They observe him: how does the candidate lay out the invoices he has to classify? They study him physiognomically and graphologically. In short, for occupational psychologists every least employee is a microcosm. Despite this high regard, gratifying in itself, for the life of the alien psyche, the union politicians present at the conference spoke out unanimously against the 'total view' practised here. With justification they question its absolute reliability; with equal justification they combat the threat character analysis poses of an encroachment into the private sphere; and finally they maintain that an at least unconscious link exists between the tester operating within the enterprise and the employer. The talents of employees, they consider, may be systematically ascertained if necessary upon entry into the job, but only in neutral locations.

Such locations are the job advice centres. The aptitude tester at one Berlin advice centre gave me an account of his own experience. It carries weight that even this man is convinced that tests have no business in the enterprise. 'Any big firm', he says, 'that needs an aptitude test in order to deploy its personnel, has poor staff supervision.' And, indeed, how little must the senior staff in an enterprise know about their juniors, if they can squeeze from them a confession of hidden talents only under scientific torture? The aptitude tester nevertheless proposes that large-scale enterprises should devise staff cards on which entries are made about their employees. The proposal, though certainly inspired by honest intentions, has hidden dangers. If the spirit of the enterprise is decent, fixed precipitates in a card-index are unnecessary; if it is poor, you will get good-conduct files whatever control mechanisms are introduced. The aptitude tester's experiences relate to shorthand typists, ledger-clerks, German- and foreign-language correspondence clerks and section managers. He loyally avoids all statements about the private individual and confines himself purely to occupational psychology. Thus on one occasion, for example, he delivers the judgement: 'In his work Herr X is a phoney.' So much for Herr X. Perhaps in private dealings with girls he inclines rather to bashfulness, but his work is all show. Should we carve the man into two halves? In order to allay my doubts, the aptitude tester informs me of some notable successes. One large firm approached him with a request to test two gentlemen, both ready to be section managers but only one of whom could fill the post that had fallen vacant. He provided an individual profile of both delinquents, in which one of them was credited with a better overview than the other. The large firm chose the better overview and is now extremely satisfied. Then the following case: a boss sent the aptitude tester two girls, one with rickets and the other as pretty as a picture. The boss would have preferred, of course, to hire the pretty one but, as so often with girls, it was the one with rickets who was the jewel. The aptitude tester, in the guise of a latterday Paris, picked not the Aphrodite but the Athene (no Hera was present among the employees). He scored a triumph when the boss, after a certain time, engaged the rickety goddess in his private office. And even in a case 'with strings' science was victorious, with the favoured candidate being rejected because of his psychologically proven unfitness. Finally the aptitude tester rounds things off by tracing my own profile, which he has put together unobtrusively during our conversation. He is a skilled observer, in whose wide-meshed web of categories certain structural features do get caught. In my case, they might suffice to classify me in an average earnings group.

Reliable experts like this are all the more important in view of the fact that aptitude tests are coming into vogue for salaried employees too. One of the proprietors of a famous specialist company explains to me how his firm proceeds in the matter of new appointments. Every applicant has to fill out a questionnaire and is personally examined by the appropriate manager. Switchboard operators and candidates for the advertising department are regarded also as natural subjects for industrial psychology. In the case of qualified staff, graphological evidence is called for. The graphologist entrusted with such expertise penetrates the employees' souls like a government spy in hostile territory. Both are supposed by secret paths to procure from the enemy camp material of value to their principals. The growing use of methods of psychological exploration, made in the service of more intensive profitability, is thus not least also a sign of the estrangement imposed by the prevailing system between employers and numerous categories of employees. Where a total view is demanded, no one really looks at each other any more. Things will probably get better only if the prophetic words of the O. and Partners announcement come true and the right people reach the right places.

That girl with rickets who found her way to the private office thanks to the aptitude tester was exceptionally favoured by Providence. For

usually today outward appearance plays a decisive role, and in order to
be rejected you need not even have rickets. 'With the huge supply of
labour', writes the Social-Democrat deputy Dr Julius Moses, 'a certain
physical "selection" inevitably occurs. Conspicuous bodily imperfec-
tions, though they may not in the least impair fitness for work,
prematurely force socially vulnerable people out of work and into
invalidity' (*Afa-Bundeszeitung*, February 1929). That this is so, and not
just with employees who come into direct contact with the public, is
confirmed from many sides. An official in a Berlin job centre explains
to me how people with physical defects – people who limp, for instance,
or even who write lefthanded – are regarded as disabled and are
particularly hard to place. They are frequently retrained. The official
makes no bones about the reduced marketability of wrinkles and grey
hair. I try to learn from him what magical properties a person's
appearance must possess in order to open the gates of the firm. The
terms 'nice' and 'friendly' recur like stock phrases in his reply. Above
all employers want to receive a nice impression. People who appear
nice – and nice manners are naturally part of the appearance – are
taken on even if their references are poor. The official says: 'We have
to do things the same way as the Americans do. The man must have a
friendly face.' In order to increase the man's friendliness, the job centre
incidentally requires him to apply with shaven cheeks and in his best
suit. The works-council chairman of one big firm likewise recommends
employees to turn out in the martial trappings of their Sunday best
when their boss is coming for a visit. One piece of information that I
obtain in a well-known Berlin department store is particularly instructive: 'When taking on sales and office staff', says an influential gentleman from the personnel department, 'we attach most importance to a
pleasant appearance.' From a distance he looks a bit like Reinhold
Schünzel in early films.[3] I ask him what he understands by 'pleasant' –
saucy or pretty. 'Not exactly pretty. What's far more crucial is . . . oh,
you know, a morally pink complexion.'

I do know. A morally pink complexion – this combination of concepts
at a stroke renders transparent the everyday life that is fleshed out by
window displays, salary-earners and illustrated papers. Its morality must
have a pink hue, its pink a moral grounding. That is what the people
responsible for selection want. They would like to cover life with a
varnish concealing its far-from-rosy reality. But beware, if morality
should penetrate beneath the skin, and the pink be not quite moral
enough to prevent the eruption of desires! The gloom of unadorned

3. Reinhold Schünzel (1888–1954) specialized in portraying elegant villains on stage
and screen; he was Tiger Brown in Pabst's 1931 *Dreigroschenoper*.

morality would bring as much danger to the prevailing order as a pink that began to flare up immorally. So that both may be neutralized, they are tied to one another. The same system that requires the aptitude test also produces this nice, friendly mixture; and the more rationalization progresses, the more the morally pink appearance gains ground. It is scarcely too hazardous to assert that in Berlin a salaried type is developing, standardized in the direction of the desired complexion. Speech, clothes, gestures and countenances become assimilated and the result of the process is that very same pleasant appearance, which with the help of photographs can be widely reproduced. A selective breeding that is carried out under the pressure of social relations, and that is necessarily supported by the economy through the arousal of corresponding consumer needs.

Employees must join in, whether they want to or not. The rush to the numerous beauty salons springs partly from existential concerns, and the use of cosmetic products is not always a luxury. For fear of being withdrawn from use as obsolete, ladies *and* gentlemen dye their hair, while forty-year-olds take up sports to keep slim. 'How can I become beautiful?' runs the title of a booklet recently launched on to the market; the newspaper advertisements for it say that it shows ways 'to look young and beautiful both now and for ever'. Fashion and economy work hand in hand. Most people, of course, are in no position to consult a specialist. They fall prey to quacks or have to make do with remedies as cheap as they are dubious. For some time now the above-mentioned deputy Dr Moses has been fighting in their interest in parliament, for incorporating proper provision for disfigurement into social security. The young Arbeitsgemeinschaft kosmetisch tätiger Ärzte Deutschlands [Working Community of Cosmetic Practitioners of Germany] has associated itself with this legitimate demand.

# Short break for ventilation

The commercial director of a modern factory explains the business to me before my tour of inspection. 'The commercial operation of the work process', he says, 'is rationalized down to the last detail.' He points to diagrams whose colourful networks of lines illustrate the whole operation. The plans hang in frames on the walls of his room. On the other wall there are two peculiar cases that look a bit like children's abacuses. Within them little brightly coloured balls, arranged on vertical cords, rise in close formation to varying heights. One glance at them, and the director at once knows all about the firm's current situation. Every couple of days the little balls are repositioned by a statistics clerk. No sound penetrates the room, there are hardly any papers on the desk. This treetop calm seems to prevail everywhere in the higher spheres. One captain of industry I know lives in monastic seclusion in the midst of the giant enterprise over which he has to hold sway; and the boss of one important firm uses light signals to inform visitors waiting at the outer door of his private office whether they should enter, wait or move on. I recall the days of mobilization, when it was said that the minister of war, thanks to the organizational miracle of deployment plans prepared in advance, sat in his peaceful office with nothing to do while outside his troops were on the march. Admittedly, the war itself was then lost ... 'Do you know what tour tickets look like?' the commercial director asked me. I nodded in astonishment. 'I'll show you our own tour tickets.' We enter a room whose iron shelves hold countless booklets that really do look just like tour tickets. They contain, folded together, all the dockets needed for carrying out the work process. The work process: i.e. the sum of functions to be performed from the arrival of the order to the dispatch of the commissioned goods. Once the order begins its journey, the route it has to follow is determined by means of the dockets; and certainly no concert agency could fix a virtuoso's tour in advance more precisely.

The equipment in the office of the manager, who has to supervise the entire tourist traffic, bears about the same resemblance to the freely invented office equipment in Fritz Lang's spy film as a fantastic sunset does to a genuine oleograph. A cupboard-like centrepiece studded with coloured light-bulbs forms the principal ornament of the real office. In general, the sole purpose today of red, yellow and green tints is to organize an enterprise more rationally. From the flashing and dimming of the tiny bulbs, the manager can at all times deduce the state of work in the individual departments. In the course of the tour through the offices that the commercial director makes with me, we gradually pace out the network of lines on the wall of his room. The marvellous thing is that the operation of the plan is set in motion by real people. A number of girls are evenly distributed about the room at Powers machines, punching cards and writing. The Powers (or Hollerich) machinery, used for bookkeeping and every kind of statistical purpose, performs by mechanical means feats whose accomplishment had previously required a never wholly reliable intellectual labour, as well as incomparably more time. The chosen instrument of machine processing is the punch-card covered with rows of figures, upon which operationally important items can be represented in numbers. Each card is perforated with the help of the punching machine and then contains the record file in perforation code. Once the cards are ready, they travel to the sorting and tabulating machines in the adjoining room. In a trice the former arrange the material according to the various items, while the latter write down the perforated numbers in the desired tabular form and add up the columns automatically. Gentlemen tend the heavy monsters, whose racket vastly surpasses the monotonous clatter of the punching girls. I ask the office manager about the machine-girls' work routine.

'The girls', he replies, 'punch for only six hours and during the remaining two hours are employed as office clerks. In this way we avoid overtaxing them. All this takes place in a predetermined cycle, so that each employee encounters all tasks. For hygienic reasons, moreover, from time to time we slip in short breaks for ventilation.'

What a scheme – even ventilation outlets are not forgotten.

'We worked for nine months on the whole system', the commercial director comments. The office manager holds a thick folio under my nose, in which the work plan applicable to the machine room is entered accurately to the minute.

'If ever, Heaven forbid, you suddenly fall ill', I said to the office manager, 'can someone else take your place at once and assume control with the help of this book?'

'Yes, of course.'

He feels tremendously flattered because his foresight in contriving to be replaceable at all times is recognized.

> And after all it's just the same
> If it's you or if it's me.

Then we move to the wages and personnel department, in which all kinds of pre-printed forms are fed through the accounting-machine.

The big banks and other big firms in which expensive investment pays have mainly gone over to proper mechanization. The commercial advantages of machine methods can hardly be overestimated; to take just one example, they enable the current-account departments of banks today to make up accounts in the shortest possible time and update them hourly. Thanks to the intellectual labour invested in the equipment, its handmaidens are spared the possession of knowledge; if attendance at commercial college were not compulsory, they would need to know nothing at all. The mysteries of the firm too are a closed book to them, since they deal only with figures. Just one thing is required of them: attention. This cannot wander free but is under the control of the apparatus it controls and – what with the noise in the machine-rooms – the less enticing the object at which it is to be directed, the more it must demand of the nerves. Some people complain about the insufficient allowance made for fatigue in the computation of tasks to be executed. There are others, of course, who commend this very strain as particularly delightful. One person, for example, writes triumphantly about the fact that machines work fast, then goes on: 'yet they cannot be operated absent-mindedly, but force their operatives to bring even their brains to an appropriate "frequency". And that is the decisive thing: work thus acquires a tempo and therewith, in my view, that which endows even a monotonous job with charm.' The enthusiasm becomes more understandable if you learn that it has been culled from a company newspaper known to sceptical employees as the 'Slime-Trumpet'. How arduous protracted mechanical activity really is may be deduced indirectly from the fact that several firms I know, like the one described above, confine it to a fraction of the working day and pay machine staff almost exclusively by means of special allowances. The fact that they are so fond of placing girls in charge of machines is due, among other things, to the innate dexterity of the young creatures – which natural gift is, however, too widely distributed, alas, to warrant a high rate of pay. When the middle classes were still in a state of prosperity, many girls who now punch cards used to stumble through *études* at home on the pianoforte. Music at least has not entirely vanished from a process that the National Board for Economic Viability has defined as follows: 'Rationalization is the application of all means offered by technology and systematic organization to the raising of economic viability, and therewith to increasing the production of goods, reducing their cost and also improving them.' No, it has not quite gone. I know of one industrial plant that hires girls straight from high school with a salary and lets them be trained at the typewriter by a teacher of their own. The wily teacher winds up a gramophone and the pupils have to type in time with its tunes. When merry military marches ring out, they all march ahead twice as lightly. The rotation speed of the record is gradually increased, and without the girls really noticing it they tap faster and faster. In their training years they turn into speed typists – music has wrought the cheaply purchased miracle.

The National Board for Economic Viability's definition has no place for the term 'human beings'. Presumably it has been forgotten because it no longer plays any very important role. Yet employees are continually to be found who register its elimination as a loss. Not so much the young ones, who grow up – or perhaps grow smaller – in the modern firm, as the older ones who can remember the former state of affairs. The chief clerk of one bank, to be sure, tells me how one of his subordinates, who initially would not hear a word about rationalization, spontaneously changed his attitude after six months; but I also know of another case, where a bank employee who had been moved to a machine was up and away after two days without any apology. The works-council chairman of one big bank speaks to me with considerable resignation about the loss of what he calls the value of personality. His personality requirements are as laughable as they are modest. Today, he tells me, the keeper of an account has basically only to 'tick off', and with limited sources of error the time he takes can be verified precisely. Formerly things were different. Then a chief clerk was a man of experience, who often needed long days to balance accounts, and might take the opportunity if he liked for private leisure, without having to fear any surveillance. So, in the opinion of the works-council chairman, the value of personality actually consists in being able to stretch work by your own decision – a conception that at least compromises far less the idealistic concept of personality still lurking among us than do the convictions of university professor Kalveram. In an essay in the journal of the German association of bank officials, Professor Kalveram denies that mechanized office work carries the danger of dehumanization. He further maintains that tending a machine requires a person's full intellectual involvement, and then explains: 'In the German view, work must lead to an unfolding and realization of one's own personality. It must be viewed as service to the great tasks of the national community to which we belong.' Nothing stands in sharper opposition to these ideologically biased impositions of Professor Kalveram than his own statement, made at another point in the same essay, that the field of activity of the masses employed in mechanized firms has been narrowed down. For many categories of employee, freedom of action has indeed been restricted as a result of rationalization. In one big bank, in which I am assured that responsibility does still lie with the chief clerk, the office manager is known nowadays as the 'corporal' – a jocular definition testifying to his diminished significance. A personnel manager is only expressing in his own way the change of functions when, in conversation with me, he says it does no harm if low- and middle-level employees specialize. The specialization process has happened in a whole number of sectors. Buyers, for instance, have had to surrender some of their independence because of increasing rationalization of the market, and supervisors once entrusted with technical management today perform precisely delimited functions in the production process. As one expert reports, the old supervisors look down on their new-style colleagues in the same way as a craftsman does on a worker. The diminution of their authority and their increased fungibility were responsible in no small measure for the fact that the supervisors' union in due course joined precisely the Afa-Bund. But what is the use of prating about personality, if work is increasingly becoming a fragmentary function?

Under these conditions it is hard to foster job satisfaction. An article in the journal of the Gewerkschaftsbund der Angestellten does indeed decree with enviable optimism: 'The science of psychology concerned with work and workers will have to seek and find paths to job satisfaction.' However, science cannot in the end be made into an all-purpose handmaiden either. At one moment it is supposed to rationalize firms and at another to create the cheerful mood that it has rationalized away. This is definitely asking too much. More sensible are attempts to revive joy in work through better promotion prospects and higher salaries – even if Professor Kalveram holds the view that in no way does 'the question of pay alone determine the attitude of individuals to their work'. But, as will be noted later, narrow limits are placed today upon the implementation of such proposals. To ideologues among the employers, job satisfaction is primarily a matter of inner nature, of course. One of them becomes downright metaphysical on the theme. Every job, he tells me approximately, has its pleasures: a roadsweeper, say, can make his activity into something quite unique. I reply that the roadsweeper takes pleasure in his uniqueness only if it gets the proper outward recognition. Even artists grow bitter if their genius remains unnoticed. That employer has a staunch ally in Professor Ludwig Heyde, the editor of *Social Praxis*, whose theory of the joys of monotony has no rival. It is simply unique, and since I see no possibility of helping any unique roadsweeper to well-earned reward and honour, I shall at least preserve this unique theory from extinction. It is designed for workers, but holds equally for many salaried employees. Professor Heyde in one paper (included in the anthology *Strukturwandlungen der deutschen Volkswirtschaft* ['Structural changes in the German national economy']) recalls recent research into monotony which came to the conclusion that many people suffer greatly in monotonous work, whereas others feel quite all right in it. Professor Heyde writes here in conclusion:

> One must not fail to appreciate, you see, that through the monotony of an unchanging activity thoughts are set free for other objects. Then the worker thinks of his class ideals, perhaps secretly calls all his enemies to account or worries about his wife and children. In the meantime, however, his work goes ahead. The female worker, especially so long as she still believes like a young girl that employment for her is only a transitory phenomenon, dreams during monotonous work of teenage novels, film dramas or betrothals; she is almost less susceptible to monotony even than the male.

One must not fail to appreciate, you see, that behind these pastoral meditations there undoubtedly lies the pipedream that workers might really think about their class ideals only in secret. How pleasant, in comparison with that professorial stuffiness, seem the candid remarks recently uttered by a factory director during a pay negotiation. The factory director told the representative of the employees' organization how he was convinced that the life of a commercial employee – a bookkeeper, say – was one of dreadful monotony, and how he himself would hardly be able to come to terms with such an existence. He did later add that those affected by monotony did not seem to find their lot so hard to bear, since he had nowhere found any numb despair. The fact that his disdain also served to belittle the demands directed to him does not invalidate his words.

Many leading figures in business and industry warn against exaggerated ideas about the usefulness of machinery, and many enterprises, especially small or medium ones, certainly refuse any violent rationalization. For the same reason, however, with growing concentration the mechanization of employees' work will make advances. How do employees themselves judge this development? Even if (including their more radical unions) in the ideological sphere they often evade the situation that confronts them instead of analysing it, they will still not sweeten with the wisdom of university professors the pills they have to swallow. One little miss typist, working in an enterprise far too big for her, tells me boldly to my face that neither she nor her colleagues are exactly wedded to the clatter of machines. The various unions are anyway desirous of bringing the full benefits of rationalization to the employees, and they know from the history of social movements that nothing is more mistaken than machine-breaking. 'The machine', one works-council member tells me, 'must be an instrument of liberation.' He has probably often heard the phrase at meetings. Its triteness makes it all the more touching.

# Enterprise within the enterprise

'I ... make the preliminary observation that I intended to submit the adduced complaints to the firm's management before I was dismissed without notice, since I am firmly convinced that the top brass were not informed as to the true facts.' The writer of this sentence, which comes from a petition lodged with the Labour Court, is a dispossessed petit bourgeois. Before the war, he was in charge of quite a large staff; after the war, he had to support himself as a disabled commercial clerk. But that is not important here. Irrelevant too that his dismissal occurred because of a two-day unexplained absence. No, the decisive thing is purely and simply that the top brass were not informed as to the true facts. Who placed himself like a wall between them and the facts? The petitioner's superior, who is not even a departmental manager. In the petition this man, a kind of deputy manager, is said to have constantly ridiculed and bullied his subordinate. 'We'll break your spirit for you', the deputy manager threatened. Or: 'We'll soon have you out of here.' The insults must have stung terribly, since they are all numbered and recorded for eternity. One learns that the tormentor frequently compelled his victim to work according to wrong instructions; described him – humiliated as he already was anyway – as a malingerer; incited him against the departmental manager and the latter against him. As can be seen from the documents of the case, the office monster tormented the petitioner's colleagues too. If one of them made a move to complain, he would at once declare: 'I deny everything.' And people kept quiet out of fear. In despair the petitioner then began to drink and came to work irregularly. 'I'm even ready for an amicable agreement', he writes in conclusion, 'but not if Mr X (the deputy manager) remains with the firm' – a phrase in which the sense of personal honour of the petit bourgeois seeks to obtain satisfaction at least on paper. At the final session of the hearing before the Labour Court, one of the top brass appeared to represent the firm. He knew neither the deputy manager – active in an outlying department – nor the plaintiff, and he expressed his astonishment at the fact that the latter had not appealed directly to head office. Perhaps this gentleman did not even belong to the highest levels of the company. The firm is known as a decent one.

If literature usually imitates reality, here it precedes reality. The works of Franz Kafka give a definitive portrait of the labyrinthine human big firm – as awesome as the pasteboard models of intricate robber-baron castles made for children – and the inaccessibility of the supreme authority. The complaint of the impoverished petit bourgeois, whose very language seems borrowed from Kafka, undoubtedly concerns an extreme case; yet it points with extreme accuracy to the typical place occupied by the mid-level boss – i.e. usually the head of department – in the modern large-scale enterprise. His position, comparable to that of a low-ranking military commander, is so important because relations between the spheres of the firm have become even more abstract through rationalization than they already were. The more systematic its organization, the less people have to do with one another. It is scarcely possible for senior staff to know anything about the employees in the lower regions, even less possible from these regions to see to the top. The departmental manager, who receives instructions and passes them on, plays the role of mediator. If he made contact as directly up above as with his subordinates, people would at least be associated through him. But where are those top brass who have the real responsibility? Even the director, upon whom the departmental manager depends, mostly finds himself today in a dependent position and, when he wishes to humble himself, is fond of calling himself an employee. Above him come the board of directors and the representatives of the banks, and the summit of the hierarchy is lost in the dark skies of finance capital. The high-ups have withdrawn so far that they are no longer touched by life down below and can make their decisions purely on the basis of economic considerations. Perhaps these require increased performance to be squeezed from one department, and the departmental manager must see to it that the requirement is met. The behest may possibly imply hardship; however, the high-ups do not know the staff. The departmental manager, who does know them, for his part will perhaps not risk his own position. It may safely be assumed that not just he, but also the big shots, are relatively amicably disposed – yet inhuman actions do not fail to materialize. They are a necessary result of the abstractness of the prevailing economy, which is moved by motives that seek to escape the real dialectic with the people kept busy in the business.

The head of one employee union closely associated with the Democratic Party tells me of his experiences. Only an unusually talented departmental manager, in his view, will dare to protest against bad measures on the board's part. Normal departmental managers do not do so. He also tells of subnormal louts who demand to be treated with servility and threaten the less obsequious elements with being marked down for dismissal. 'Particular care should be taken', he concludes, 'in the selection of departmental managers.' It is more than doubtful whether this admonition is followed, particularly by those large-scale enterprises that like to install former officers as departmental managers. Where military discipline is in vogue, the danger does at least arise that you will find a lot of 'cycling'. 'Cyclists' is a term often used for officers who bow down to those above them and trample those below. Luckily things are not stuffy everywhere. A works-council member from one bank extols the comradely relationship that exists there between the upper and nether regions. And the employee of an insurance company, an elderly man seeking in vain to hide his wretchedness behind a schoolmaster's beard, claims to have noticed that young people today behave somewhat more freely towards their office superiors than before. Were it not for his beard, his wretchedness would long since have done for him. Some small part of the pressures exerted, by the way, may be due to the overabundant supply of workers and the present-day shortage of openings.

The construction of the employee hierarchy is bound up with the mentality of the employers. If they adopt the *Herr-im-Haus* [master-in-the-house] attitude, the departmental managers too will be little masters. In a certain company, well organized in the military style, the appeals procedure has to be strictly adhered to for complaints. So, if their employees knuckle under or develop into dedicated climbers, the bosses probably think everything is fine – but that is what the wielders of power thought in imperial Germany too. More far-sighted, at all events, are those far from exceptional employers who know how to compromise in their own interest, and who build in safety valves through which dissatisfaction can dissipate. In order to counter the arbitrariness of junior managers, the head of personnel in a certain huge company some time ago removed the customary plaque 'Admission by previous appointment only' hanging on his door, but can in principle be spoken to by all employees without advance formalities. Immediately after the introduction of this measure, it seems the staff poured into his room in such crowds that he had to yell and drive them away like a flock of evil spirits. And although today only four or five individuals still make use of the direct right of complaint, those few are mostly in the right. The valve should simply not be opened too wide. Elsewhere office managers are urged to write reports on their subordinates according to a specified model. If, as happens from time to time, employees then move from one department to another, comparison of their reports affords a certain possibility of checking the reliability of their direct superiors. Or a certain breathing-space is created for employees in the lower regions by introducing a letterbox into the establishment, into which proposals for company improvements may be posted without any need for a counter-signature. 'All those who submit proposals', we learn from one company newspaper, 'by doing so demonstrate their interest in working together with the firm.' So the letterbox kills two birds with one stone.

'The training of our commercial recruits', it is noted in one business expert's essay on the rationalization of commercial organizations, 'in so far as it seeks to foster the human and personal development of young people by setting new and deeper aims, forms a powerful counterweight against the dangers, arising from the rationalization of office work, of one-sided working methods within a very narrow range of duties.' In this sentence, the admission that with growing specialization the mass of employees becomes more and more one-sided is significant. 'Unfortunately the horizon of bank employees has become narrower today', laments a bank official who formerly thought it broad; and quite a number of employers tell me in this connection how they see a danger in the one-sidedness of young employees. If they try to counter this, however, it is least of all for the sake of 'human and personal development'. On the contrary, those in authority see to the training of young recruits mainly because it is demanded by the same economic logic that imposes the mechanization of labour. 'Intensive human cultivation is necessary', one leading businessman tells me, who certainly does not have an exactly human intensity in mind. If senior staff are needed, they must be bred. Since the more work is fragmented into different functions, the harder it becomes to find such staff, a whole series of large firms are undertaking the task of educating their members themselves. Workplace schools are becoming common, and grants are provided for attending continuation courses. The personnel manager of one big bank explains to me the arrangements in his firm, which, however, serve not so much what the above-mentioned essay rather enthusiastically terms 'new and deeper aims' as the particular requirements of the employer. Once all apprentices have been rough-hewn in compulsory company classes, the ablest among them – about whom the personnel department is informed – can take part along with younger employees in courses in which they gain their final polish personally from departmental managers and directors. Other firms no doubt proceed similarly; I certainly know of some that send young people for whom it makes commercial sense through the various departments and abroad. The publicity brochure of one department store mentions the education of staff no longer of school age, and explains in this connection: 'Particular mention may be made here of the periodically held staff "conferences", which are extremely important especially before major events.' The high-sounding word 'conferences' is unfortunately qualified by inverted commas, which are presumably intended to prevent the deeper aims of such conferences from being mistaken for the still deeper ones of the board of directors. Things do not go so splendidly in all companies, of course, by a long chalk. One expert maintains that far too little is done for those who have completed their apprenticeship, even though commercial ability usually develops only in your twenties; and the observation of one official is certainly correct, that employees frequently grow old and grey in their posts without any further training.

All training aims by its very nature at the further progress of the trained. In reality the chances of promotion are faint. Many who during the inflation or before it had reached almost the top – as confidential clerks, for example – have even been shunted downstairs again. Now they have to die down there. The fact that people at machines, as one bank director serenely admits to me, have no real career ahead of them, could at least be to the advantage of other categories of employee. Yes, if the chances of moving up did not depend upon the conjuncture, the employers' side explains. Thoughtful employees connect their worsened career prospects with the present generational stratification, with mechanization, and with the concentration process. The number of candidates has increased, one of them finds; while an elderly technician opines: 'Before the change-over there were ten or twelve drawing-offices where now there is only one. Management wants to negotiate with as few people as possible.' In return, it is sometimes itself more than overstaffed – to which that wretched little fellow from the insurance company with his bristling beard draws attention. Only bank reports do not usually disclose what share of staff costs is allotted to senior management.

But all these reasons do not suffice to explain the fact that the employees of a firm scarcely ever scale its summit. It certainly does happen that some former office-boy, thanks to his exceptional abilities, progresses to being an independent representative of a public corporation; and that on occasion a managing director rises from the ranks and is forever held up before the masses as an example. The above-mentioned department-store publicity brochure is also permitted to sing the firm's praises with the almost rhapsodic words: 'Many ladies have . . . worked their way up even to the position of buyer. Certainly a success that would otherwise be difficult or impossible for them to attain in civil life.' What difference, however, do individual cases make to the norm? Ordinary employees, officials, works-council members and deputies assure me that senior posts almost without exception are filled not from within the enterprise itself, but from outside; and one union leader, who from professional optimism usually paints things only in glowing colours, bombards me with examples that all demonstrate how well-born or socially acceptable these outsiders are. Indeed, one of the most influential figures in German economic life tells me straight out about a mafia at the top. 'You're in it', he says, 'by birth, through social connections, thanks to the recommendation of senior officials and important clients; rarely as a result of achievements within the firm. Young people belonging to this protected elite are installed in the firm for one purpose alone, to prepare them for their prospective future on the general staff. Their career is spent in any case inside the clique, which for the most part is recruited from within itself and, with its splendid income, stands out sharply from the crowd. If someone does actually drop out, care is taken of him; and many posts are sinecures.'

Not often is someone as absent-minded when parrying such charges as the retired bank director who, in a backward glance at his beginnings, states almost verbatim: 'I did not have any connections at all through family or friends with the world of business or banking', and then a bit later continues: 'An uncle in Berlin who had banking connections took me to see K, a director of the X bank . . . After a short test Mr K told me I could join it.' The company newspaper that prints this somewhat senile mélange of old age and daydreaming (it is the 'Slime-Trumpet', already quoted earlier), in its need to humbug its readership with an unqualified success story, obviously did not notice the contradiction at all. Far removed from such self-revealing naivety is the frequently heard complaint of employers that there is a shortage of good young recruits. Young people are allegedly not interested in improving themselves and do not want to take on any responsibility. Even assuming that the mass of employees of the post-war generation are really as apathetic as they are claimed to be, they are so not least because they have to work for the most part in conditions that make them apathetic. Because narcotics and distractions of every kind – as will be discussed later – constantly lull them. Because, in many of them and not the most worthless, awareness of their limited chances – supposedly a result of their reputed indolence – prematurely destroys all ambition.

# Alas, so soon!

Opposite the Kaiser Wilhelm Memorial Church, where the Gloriapalast and the Marmorhaus salute each other like proud castles on the Dardanelles,[4] there recently stood a man who had hung a plaque around his own neck. The man made a pitiful impression, the plaque told fragments of his autobiography. From the text written in bold characters passers-by could discover that the man was a 25-year-old unemployed salesman who was seeking work on the open market – no matter what kind. Hopefully he has found some – but it does not seem likely. The key question: was the man young or old? To judge by a newspaper advertisement quoted in the GdA journal, he is already to be classified as an older employee. For in the advertisement a menswear store wants an older salesman of twenty-five or twenty-six. If it goes on like this, babies will soon be included among the younger ones. But even if the menswear store may cultivate an exaggerated notion of youth, the age limit in business life today really has moved sharply downwards, and at forty many who still think themselves hale and hearty are, alas, economically already dead.

Retrenchment has put a premature end to them. 'Typical of our age', writes the aforementioned GdA journal (no. 5, 1929), which generally stands up in particular for older employees, 'are the very frequently recurring reports that only younger staff is being taken on and all older employees are being got rid of.... The reports come precisely to a large extent from younger employees.' Or, as is explained in the recently published memorandum of the Union of German Employer Associations on 'The labour market situation of older employees':

> The readjustment of individual firms, and the reorganization of firms' management structure in connection with rationalization measures, have

4. Berlin picture palaces among those celebrated in Kracauer's 1926 essay 'Cult of Distraction', see *The Mass Ornament*, pp. 323–8.

naturally also made necessary the dismissal of a few older workers; this may have had differing consequences according to the diverse structure of individual firms or individual industrial groups, but it was unavoidable in the interest of maintaining those firms' profitability.

Alas, they have thoroughly rationalized even the language! Incidentally the memorandum, which modestly speaks only of *a few* employees, still attributes retrenchment to the difficulties suffered by the economy thanks to the influx, during the war and the inflation, of formerly self-employed elements and numerous unskilled people. The unskilled have for the most part been got rid of again. The general motives for retrenchment should, in any case, be complemented by some special ones that precisely urge the axing of older people. Perhaps rationalization must usually proceed over more elderly corpses precisely because these are entitled to the highest rates of pay. Furthermore most of them are married, explains the social-policy adviser of one large employee union, and are entitled to benefits; but mechanized work can be coped with equally well by workers who are single and enjoy the good fortune of youth.

There are both fast and slow methods of retrenchment. These fine nuances may well be of no consequence, compared with the fact of retrenchment; but to ignore them would be all the more inappropriate in that, even according to the employers' memorandum, it is always a matter of just a few employees. In one big bank not long ago, a number of machine-girls were sent letters of dismissal whose brevity was in inverse proportion to their length of service. With girls punching cards, you generally rely on 'natural wastage'; in other words, you wait for them to leave the firm of their own accord, when they feel old age approaching. Although those dismissed were already past thirty, they were not budging an inch. Was it perhaps their intention to wear themselves out with never-ending holes for long enough to ensure extra remuneration? They were offered generous compensation, but they will hardly find a job again in their old age. One of them is thirty-nine and all she possesses apart from the compensation is an invalid mother. However, their own foolishness is often to blame for the girls' misfortune. Since they can manage quite tolerably on a salary augmented by office bonuses, they shrink from any marriage in which they would do worse materially. If they are subsequently made redundant, they get neither a new job nor a husband. Sometimes the procedure takes place as if in slow motion. In order to defer the final dismissal, one bank stores all those made redundant in a reserve department, where it tries to employ them profitably for a while. Under favourable circumstances people even move from the storehouse back into banking life. The

reader will assuredly still recall the girls mentioned earlier, who had
trained as speed typists to the sounds of a gramophone. They were
released into the office and, at the first go, out-typed all their elder
colleagues. Since the latter had no music in their bodies, they forfeited
the bonuses paid out to the fire of youth. Finally the firm lost patience
with them and put them once more at the disposal of the personnel
department, which offered them to the clerical office, whose manager
likewise, however, preferred to take the brisker gramophone girls. So
they gradually ended up outside.

Different categories of employee are differently affected by retrenchment. Certainly old age is always poorly construed, but technical
employees nevertheless tolerate a greater strain than do commercial
ones. 'In accounts offices', a qualified engineer explains to me, 'you
need experienced people and have no time for pushy young gentlemen
who merely annoy the workers in the shop with their unreasonable
demands.' He is admittedly an elderly accountant himself. Tallying with
his information, the foremen organized in the Werkmeisterverband are
on average over fifty years old. Companies too have not all rejuvenated
with the same enthusiasm. A specialist firm, for instance, in which what
matters is individual treatment of customers, is not in the least
interested in rapid staff turnover but wants to retain practised employees for as long as possible. A couple of department stores I know are
just as far from scorning the wisdom of old age. The personnel manager
of one department store – the same one who recommended a morally
pink complexion as an advantage – attempts to confirm that they also
honour it, by alluding to the speech meted out to every member of the
firm after twenty-five years' service. The speech is accompanied by a
present. Not least, there are quite a few big banks and industrial
concerns that have given up the idea of transforming themselves
suddenly into youth hostels. 'We can, of course, not carry the burden
for ever of downright semi- or total idiots', said the personnel manager
of one such banking institute to the works-council chairman, on the
occasion of the dismissal of veterans who – as the works-council
chairman in turn told me – had originally got in by patronage. Ageing
takes place most comfortably, it may be assumed, in the realm of senior
management, whose inhabitants know how to protect themselves
against dismissal by means of long-term contracts and the guarantee of
sizeable compensation payments. Atmospheric discharges in firms are
almost never high-altitude storms.

The real tempest of rationalization is over, but 'at the present
moment in time, however, the measures have not yet been conclusively
carried through', as the employers' associations write. Companies are
constantly being merged, departments disbanded or amalgamated. If

immobility is death, this movement in no way signifies life for older employees. Firms do proceed more cautiously than before, though, because among other things they fear Social-Democrat attacks; and even the employers' memorandum promises: 'when redundancies become necessary, and also when posts are refilled, to improve the position of older employees within the bounds of what is economically possible.' Thus one bank, which in the summer was getting ready for new redundancies, promised the works council that it would not eliminate older employees unless necessary. But what if it does become necessary? It was confirmed to me from many quarters that precisely bank employees, above all those of advanced age, suffer from a lack of existential security. 'Their mood is depressed', says one of them, 'because the Damocles' sword of dismissal is suspended over them.' Another formulates it in less cultivated fashion: 'Formerly everybody thought they had a job for life, today they're afraid of redundancy.' Now they feel how things are for workers.

Society at large has sought to limit the hardship of older employees by means of the law against wrongful dismissal and various other measures. But certain proposals made by the employee unions, whose realization might have limited the private initiative of employers, had to remain unfulfilled: for instance, the demand for older people to get strict preferential treatment. How intractable many big firms are in the face of such a demand is shown by the following case, taken to the appeal court of the regional Labour Court. It also proves that a court may sometimes encourage what it cannot require by law. A 33-year-old shorthand typist, who had worked since 1913 in a giant industrial firm, was re-hired as a simple typist when her department was merged with another department on the grounds of rationalization. Six months later the firm dismissed the demoted employee for low output and frequent absences. The appeal court decision that followed the first verdict viewed the dismissal as unfairly harsh, in spite of those frequent absences. 'Whether the plaintiff really worked too slowly', the written statement comments on the charge of low output, 'or a particularly intensive strain was placed on her colleagues' energies, can be left open.' Of special significance here is that part of the motivation for the verdict which, in unambiguous words, lays moral responsibility upon the enterprise for an employee who has conducted herself properly for many years. The forthright clauses declare:

> Given the size and scale of the company, the court of appeal considers proven that it would have been possible for the defendant to continue employing her (i.e. the plaintiff) either as a shorthand typist, or on filing, or as a clerk in the packing department. ... This must certainly apply if an employee who

has been in the firm for fifteen years – and against whom until recently no complaint could be made in either a practical or a personal respect – does not fully comply in one position with what is asked of her. All possibilities should then have been exhausted, in order to employ her in another position in which she could carry out her work in a way that was profitable for the firm.

The former shorthand typist received compensation.

All possibilities should indeed have been exhausted, since the real misfortune of older people is that, having once been made redundant, they are unlikely to be employed again. As though they were afflicted with leprosy, the gates of the firm are barred against them. At the risk of boring the reader, I shall cite a number of replies given by unemployed people to a questionnaire organized by the Gewerkschafts-bund der Angestellten (and processed in the GdA journal on 1 February 1929).

1. Former manager with approx. 400 Reichsmark salary. Obliged to sell furniture and fur coat and let out a room. I am forty years old and married. Father of two children (boy three-and-a-half, girl six months). Unemployed since 1 April 1925.

2. Thirty-nine, married, three children (fourteen, twelve, nine). Three years earned nothing. Future? Work, madhouse, or turn on the gas.

3. Made redundant, because military candidates were taken on. I sold my furniture. Before the war several businesses of my own, which I had to give up as a result of the war and my call-up. When I came home my wife died. All my savings were stolen away by the great national fraud (inflation). Now I am fifty-one years old, so everywhere I hear: 'We don't take on people of that age.' The final step for me is suicide. The German state is our murderer.

4. I am spiritually broken and sometimes entertain thoughts of suicide. Moreover, I have lost confidence in all men. Thirty-eight years old, divorced, four children.

5. Future? Hopeless, if something is not done soon in some way or another for employees like us, older but fully trained and still quite capable of working. Forty-four, married.

6. Future hopeless and without prospects. Early death would be best. This is written by a 32-year-old [!], married and father of two children.

The employers counter these tearful confessions with an assault upon wage settlements, whose inflexibility does indeed provoke many difficulties today. 'The present structure of wage settlements, which in general automatically links the right to a higher salary for employees with increasing age', they say in their memorandum, 'in many cases forms an obstacle not to be underestimated to the recruitment of older employees.' This argument is unfortunately bound to be used. In their despair some individuals made redundant accept the peace terms of the enemy, himself often in a bad way. One of them advertised at the end of April 1929, in a widely sold daily newspaper:

*I don't give a fig for the union rates!*
I prefer pay and bread. What employer would like a reliable, versatile clerk, late forties, for in-house or regular off-site work?

Whether the man found employment is an open question. Some people seem to have surrendered in vain. At all events, one laid-off 43-year-old, who formerly had a salary of 800 Marks as an auditor and personnel manager, reports in the GdA survey mentioned above: 'Although I offer myself as an accountant and ask for only 200 Marks, all my applications are rejected.' Apparently the ones to be counted lucky are those whom a respectable settlement helps to parasitic independence. Others sell newspapers or vanish into Berlin as tram conductors.

Behind the aversion for the elderly, extremely prosaic people sense a further secret motive that they cannot comprehend. One trade-union secretary, who is the epitome of pure objectivity, ventures on to the open seas of psychology to interpret the phenomenon. 'We are dealing with a mass psychosis', he says – yes, he speaks of psychological disturbance. The disdain shown nowadays for old age does indeed go beyond its costliness. 'Young people are simply easier to deal with', is an expression frequently heard. As if older people were not even easier to deal with, if anybody would only employ them. The fact that they are treated more ruthlessly than is perhaps required, even in the interest of firms' profitability, stems in the last resort from the general abandonment of old age nowadays. Not just employers, but the whole nation has turned away from it and, in a dismaying manner, glorifies youth in itself. Youth is the fetish of illustrated newspapers and their public; older people court it and rejuvenating nostrums are supposed to preserve it. If growing old means going to meet death, then this idolization of youth is a sign of flight from death. But as death crowds in on people, the meaning of life is opened up to them for the first time; and the lines 'How fair is youth/ That ne'er returns' really mean that youth is fair because it never returns. Death and life are so intimately interwoven with one another that you cannot have the latter without the former. If old age is dethroned, therefore, youth may have won, but life has lost the game. Nothing more clearly indicates that it is not mastered than the dangling after youth – which it is a disastrous misconception to call life. The rationalized economy undoubtedly encourages, if not engenders, this misconception. The less sure it is of its meaning, the more strictly it forbids the mass of working people to ask about its meaning. But if people are not permitted to look towards a meaningful end, then the ultimate end – death – likewise eludes them. Their life, which should have been confronted with death in order to be life, is dammed and driven back to its beginnings, to youth. Youth, from which life descends, turns into its perverted fulfilment, since the genuine fulfilment is barred. The dominant economic mode does not wish to be seen through, so sheer vitality must prevail. The overrating of youth is as much a repression as the devaluation of old age, which goes beyond the bounds of necessity. Both phenomena testify indirectly to the fact that under present economic and social conditions human beings are not living life.

In so far as society is nature, it tends like all living natural forms to correct its own defects. The fact of retrenchment and warnings in the trade-union press have led to a reduced new generation of commercial employees. A legal adviser from the retail trade explains to me without hesitation that he would not let his son take up a career from which he could so easily be kicked out again. Fresh apprentice material, requested by firms from job centres and trade unions, is not always immediately available. Nor are girls always keen to come along right away either. Many of them are put off by the long working day in department stores and other firms, and prefer commercial offices that close in the afternoon while there is still daylight. Some improvement in the overall labour market during the next five years is promised, at all events, by the lower wartime birth rate. However, many economic policy-makers are of the opinion that its effect will hardly be very durable, since the shortfall in births will not match the still unabsorbed over-supply of the pre-war years for a long time to come. 'The tendency not to take on older people is continuing for the time being', asserts an expert from the job centre. He lays part of the blame on the apprentice system which, especially in retail businesses, is detrimental to mature workers. Even the more encouraging statistical considerations, alas, cannot change the fact that redundant older employees meanwhile grow older and older – and everyone lives only once.

# Repair shop

In very large companies the works-council representatives have their
own offices, in which I have never been able to avoid the tingling
feeling that I am, as it were, visiting an extra-territorial domain. You are
inside the company, of course, but outside its jurisdiction. Often these
enclaves are provided with an ante-chamber, a telephone and perhaps
even a secretary – equipment that is less menacing, however, than it
appears. 'The old dodderers were quite amazed by the proles at first':
that is how one older employee describes to me the works-council
representatives' debut on the board of directors. The old dodderers
have pulled themselves together quickly, and not infrequently have
sought to block the influence of the employees' representatives by
technical administrative measures. Important deliberations take place
nowadays in sub-committees where the bank representatives and big
shareholders are on their own. 'So under today's conditions', says an
article in the journal *Die Arbeit*, organ of the Confederation of German
Trade Unions, 'it cannot be the task of the works-council representatives
on the board of directors to speechify there, but to keep quiet and
learn as much as possible.' An official of the Allgemeine Verband der
Deutschen Bankangestellten claims to have noticed, incidentally, that it
is not always exactly the works council's ablest minds who stay on the
board of directors. Even in daily company routine, the statutory 'parallel
authority' is very unwillingly tolerated by many firms. I know one
medium-sized enterprise whose commercial manager not long ago
threatened his secretary with immediate disciplinary transfer if she let
herself be elected to the works council; she is still working as his
secretary. Unquestionably shrewder than such archaic firms are all
those companies that behave correctly towards employee representatives. They spare themselves unnecessary trouble, and probably have
sufficiently precise mastery of the works-council legislation to exploit its
weaknesses. Moreover, they know that the works council is acting partly

in the interest of the whole company when it reviews the food in the canteen or cooperates in redundancies. One big bank even views the works council as a kind of seedbed for able workers, of whom it is happy to make use. The employees of this bank, though, call the chosen ones 'careerists'. Though manifestly inspired by resentment, the term of abuse clearly indicates the difficulties to which works-council members are exposed. In firms where rationalization has taken place and they often have to play the role of mediator, they almost necessarily provoke doubts from below and temptations from above. Officials of more radical unions explain to me how they see a danger especially in the release from work enjoyed by the works-council chairmen of large-scale enterprises (a privilege that the technicians among them do not even welcome, incidentally, since they are afraid of losing touch with their vocation – which requires constant further training – during the long break). Some of these persons released from employee status are accused within their own unions of being too compliant, or of not always successfully resisting bourgeois proclivities. In one enterprise constructed with social adroitness, the works-council chairman boasts apartments that would not shame a managing director. These do not merely serve him, they are simultaneously a showpiece for important customers. The personnel manager of this company is a man of humane disposition, who really enthuses to me about his good relations with the works council. 'Our works-council members are of moderate bent', an employee of the same firm tells me.

No matter whether the employee representatives practise moderation or not, in the consolidated economy they in any case de facto have numerous repairs to carry out – sometimes, despite themselves, even where they are combating the prevailing economic order. Like Hegelian reason, this order has its ruses and for the time being is strong enough to fill with ambiguity even actions that do not accept its continued existence. This does not prevent relations between works councils and employers often breaking down. Then in certain cases repairs are made, on neutral ground in public and in the light of day. Such light disenchants physiognomies. Plaintiffs, defendants and witnesses are as bare as the hearing chamber of the Labour Court in which they assemble. No make-up brings the girls' faces into flower, and every pimple on those of the men is visible in close-up. They are like Sunday trippers in reverse: Sunday trippers torn away from their work who, rather than wandering free and self-conscious trapped out in their best clothes, have been robbed of their finery and are far away from the glamour of evening. While they talk, huddle and wait, the memory awakens of those military recruitment centres in which miserable, naked men were registered as fit for war service. The merciless light stirs the memory. Just as there it revealed not so much the nakedness as the war, so here it really reveals not wretched people but conditions that make people wretched. In its austere glow minute details emerge with unwonted clarity, which are anything but minute details: for taken together they characterize the economic life that spawns them. We must rid ourselves of the delusion that it is major events which most determine a person. He is more deeply and lastingly influenced by the tiny catastrophes of which everyday existence is made up, and his fate is certainly linked predominantly to the sequence of these miniature occurrences. They become apparent in the Labour Court, in front of the long, raised table behind which the chairman of the court is enthroned between two assessors representing employers and employees respectively. The three judges usually reach their decision at once, after a short deliberation in the cabinet separated off from the courtroom itself. Summary jurisdiction is made possible by its wholly oral character. Use of paper is limited, only the chairman knows the documents. Thanks to the directness of the question-and-answer game to which no attorney gives a final legal polish, the chairman is more dependent upon his instinct than in a regular court. The necessity of improvisation produces a kind of atmospheric tension, sometimes transmitted even to the court clerk.

The parties unpack their wares: nothing but little parcels of woe. They depict the state of affairs, reply to the chairman and his assessors, and address one another. Sometimes one party behaves as though the other were not present. As a rule the complaints are brought by people who have been sacked. For instance, dismissals without notice may be involved. That they can occur lawfully is shown by the following trifling matter. A woman buys shoes in a large store, where the plaintiff is employed – she works in the stocking department. The woman knows the plaintiff personally and would like to purchase some stockings from her to go with the shoes. The stocking-salesgirl evidently subordinates commercial interest to the personal relationship, since she tells the woman that she could have bought the shoes more cheaply elsewhere. Because of her wrong-headed worldview the girl gets the sack – and her appeal is rejected. Such lapses by employees are matched by many cases in which it is the holders of power themselves who lapse. Not infrequently a person is out on the street with no idea how it has happened. One seriously disabled sixty-year-old was dismissed on the spot because, in the presence of several witnesses, he told the 29-year-old chief clerk: 'I won't be ordered about by you.' The elderly invalid's angry little sentence was interpreted by the firm as an offence against the majesty of company discipline. One wireless store has the curious custom of subjecting its small number of employees to physical searches at frequent intervals. On the occasion of one such investigation, a notebook comes to light from the pocket of a young 'trainee' that is unquestionably his private property. The suspicious boss, without prior consultation, considers himself entitled to search the notebook for headphones and aerials. Albeit not finding the expected stolen goods, he does find a few extremely heretical jottings. For instance, the conscientious youth has recorded how some day he would like to draw the attention of the health and safety inspectorate to the firm, and has furthermore noted down the address of the Zentralverband der Angestellten. The secret rebel is dismissed without notice by the boss. However, the Labour Court decides that the material against him has been obtained on the strength of a breach of common decency, and urges a settlement.

Nasty tricks, common practices, economic relations and social conditions are not documented by the proceedings, but present themselves in them. Take testimonials, meaningless documents for the most part but upon whose wording whole existences may perhaps depend. One vocational adviser tells me that the prospects for young people made redundant worsen if their testimonial does not have the usual concluding sentence wishing them every success. 'Mr X has made a sincere effort to carry out his work satisfactorily': because of this formulation trainee X, who has been made redundant, turns for help to the appropriate official of his trade union, who asks the trainee's boss kindly to confirm that Mr X has indeed carried out his work satisfactorily. If complaints are not caught by the unions, they land up at the Labour Court, which usually forces modification of dubious documents by pointing to the hardships of the unemployed. Apart from flagrant cases, that is quite all right; for there are few offences that justify any lengthy exclusion from employment, and even fewer bosses authorized to take responsibility for such an exclusion. Complaints about wrong grading are as typical as protests about testimonials. In one instructive borderline case the plaintiff, who as a clerk in industry really counts as an industrial worker, demands retrospective compensation that he would have been entitled to expect only as a commercial employee. He used to look after a card register, or something of the sort. The firm thinks he suffers from delusions of grandeur, while the Labour Court explains that his activity is a commercial one, just like all the innumerable commercial clerks who have to perform mechanical tasks under the current rationalization. More and more often, too, victims are washed ashore whose dismissal is connected with mergers and other stormy events in the upper regions. The fact that many firms really do find themselves in difficulties is no consolation to those who have not been involved in the big game.

Different from the mass of plaintiffs are all those employees who would like to be seen as such legally, but not socially: commercial travellers, agents on commission, insurance brokers, publicity ladies, etc. Formerly they were officers or middle-class characters of modest independence. In the rationalized world of the salaried employee, these bourgeois ruins stand out strangely with their private feelings and whole bygone inner architecture. They would probably collapse completely if they did not sustain themselves with the thought that they were once something better. Things mostly go worse for them than for other employees. In disputes over expenses and commissions they appear before the Labour Court, which as we all know also has jurisdiction with respect to 'employee-like' persons. They lodge complaints there on their own initiative, personally injured private individuals seeking above all to give both themselves and others the impression that they are socially on a par with the masters. It is as though they still dwelt in their sold-off front parlours. Which is certainly where the elderly agent emerges from, who spices his conversation with Latin quotations and tells the Labour Court, among other things, that his son is in the upper sixth. Denied his commission because an order was not given, he claims that his predecessor alone was to blame for the mishap. 'Mr Chairman', he declaims, 'King Louis XV died for the sins of his predecessor. Must I now pay for those of mine?' 'It was Louis XVI', the chairman retorts. Incidentally, dispossessed big businessmen sometimes turn up among the employees made redundant and as such demand their rights. The chief clerk of one large firm is dismissed due to differences of opinion. The firm takes the opportunity to check back every penny he has used for private purposes. For example, he took coal from the factory and had domestic repairs done by workers – all of this is now brought up against him. But perhaps the ex-chief clerk is merely paying for the sins of his father, who was somewhat similar to Louis XV: i.e. the former owner of the firm, which later passed into other hands through a merger.

Complaints follow one another in unbroken sequence. They are already sifted before they are brought forward: either by a court official in the registry or, more usually, by the employee organizations. On their way through the works council the majority of them simply come to the notice of the trade unions, whose interest is thereby engaged. From the fact that wherever works councils intervene actively they behave like union officials, one Labour Court chairman friend of mine infers the absence of company-union leanings among the employed. 'Employees', he says, 'are individualists, or they are organized in trade unions.' But it is still debatable whether, as he believes, company collectivism must fail utterly because of that. In his experience, a particularly large number of union complaints are based on Paragraph 84 of the Works Council Act, which provides for appeals against dismissals constituting undue hardship. The paragraph is of decisive significance in the event of redundancy, since with its help the unions frequently insist upon a judicial review of dismissals that have taken place. Corrections are determined by social considerations, which will be discussed later on. How is the Labour Court itself located in the social sphere? My informant, who chairs the proceedings on roughly every second day, provides me with some detail on the typical behaviour of the parties and judges. He claims to have noticed that the employee is generally more open than the employer towards proposals made to him by the court. But that is how it must be, of course, since the employee is practised in compliance and, moreover, knows perfectly well that the judges are not ill-disposed towards him even if they recommend withdrawal of his complaint. The people who appear as authorized representatives of the firm are usually employees too: head clerks and other senior persons. They defend the boss's interests with powers of persuasion not always devoid of tragi-comic effect. For a few weeks later they may find themselves on the opposite side, suing the same boss whose part they took in better days.

The assessors who along with the chairman make up the bench, though appointed by the respective associations, by no means always decide in favour of their class comrades. The employers' assessor, who is generally a big businessman, a company attorney or a senior employee, will not be very keen, for example, to express his solidarity with small tradesmen who treat their employees badly. Conversely, the employees' assessor, whose duties are usually performed by a trade-union official, is ready at any time to rap the knuckles of a foolish union brother, let alone someone not in a union. If he comes from senior employee circles, the chairman has the feeling of being hedged in by two assessors for the employers. Despite such limitations, the Labour Court today is one of the few places where formal democracy strives to fill itself with a genuine content. As it has remained a mere torso, like other institutions it can remove only minor hardships generated by the economic order.

*Labour exchanges* are reminiscent of marshalling yards, with innumerable tracks along which the jobless are shunted to and fro like wagons. They are probably the one place from which the company itself appears as a goal and a home. Since many tracks are blocked, the wagons pile up. At the job department of one employee union, the throng at the familiar window must be every box-office teller's dream; and the Berlin-Mitte labour exchange is actually an overblown big firm – or rather the negative of a big firm, since it strives to rationalize what the latter leaves unrationalized. In the office for commercial employees, one of the many in the labour exchange, I acquired an insight into the methods by which transfer of the commodity labour-power is ordered. Here it is subjected to individual treatment: in other words, people pass from the general waiting-room individually into the room of the official responsible for placing them. With the help of one of those marvellous card indexes with which all Germany is bestrewn nowadays, he works the levers of the immense signal-box. Workers are taken on piecemeal, by the way, not so much because of their individual qualities, but so that they can be more smoothly dispatched. The speed with which this is done is ensured, among other things, by the rule that every newcomer must have a letter of application ready and always to hand. If no suitable buyer is available for the commodity labour-power, perhaps someone it does not really suit will take it – the main thing is for it to be bundled off.

A lowly commercial employee once recounted to me her involuntary wanderings through the various branches. She was employed in a trading company, an arms factory, a perfumery business and several other firms, and now craves the haven of matrimony, which she considers the last resort. Her odyssey, though, was not organized by the labour exchange, but determined by newspaper advertisements, which shone out like flashing beacons to the sea-tossed woman. I asked her how she had felt while job-hunting. 'There's usually nothing else left, is there', she replied, 'and besides it makes no difference what you do, if you're not productive.' A sad answer and a false notion of productivity.

Anyone who hangs around employment offices for some time notices waste products that are hardly ever shown on public tours of the economy. There, those who have been laid off – the ones statistics report on in figures – appear in person. There, the wives of the chronically unemployed are calmed down – the ones who at home reproach their husbands with not wanting to work. The reproach, for which the tormented women should be forgiven, should under no circumstances be generalized. Laid-off workers do not go on the dole for pleasure, and cases of reluctance to work are exceptions. An hour's object lesson in the waiting-rooms of any labour exchange would be highly desirable for everybody. 'Give me some work instead – that'd be better', is the constant heartfelt sigh of the person drawing benefits. The officials entrusted with the information on jobs make every possible effort to rise above the role of passive mediators. Thus they follow movements on the labour market like meteorologists studying the weather, and detect not without regret each deep depression forming in the area of one trade or another. At least younger office clerks, bookkeepers and shorthand typists are, by all accounts, favoured by friendly air-currents these days. However, you never quite know where you are with the weather. Even if the labour exchanges rightly refrain from influencing it by means of prayers and processions, they still attempt to turn all its vagaries to account. They retrain competent workers in accordance with current requirements, cultivate their relationship with employers, and keep special employees for off-site work who check with firms for possible jobs. Older people, whom they want to dispose of at all costs, are treated like problem children and have to report to the labour exchange daily. In this way, at least, they have some occupation. Alas, if no other turns up their existence is not full enough to be worth prolonging – and some of them do then finally turn on the gas.

# A few choice specimens

Salaried employees today live in masses, whose existence – especially in Berlin and the other big cities – increasingly assumes a standard character. Uniform working relations and collective contracts condition their lifestyle, which is also subject, as will become apparent, to the standardizing influence of powerful ideological forces. All these compulsions have unquestionably led to the emergence of certain standard types of salesgirl, draper's assistant, shorthand typist and so on, which are portrayed and at the same time cultivated in magazines and cinemas. They have entered the general consciousness, which from them forms its overall image of the new salaried stratum. The question is whether the image decisively catches reality.

It is congruent with reality only in part. To be precise, it neglects in the main all those features, patterns and phenomena that arise from the clash between present-day economic necessities and a living matter that is alien to them. The life of the proletarian – and in general the 'lower' – strata of the people by no means conforms easily to the requirements of the rationalized economy. On the contrary, these are met incomparably better by the formal culture native to the genuine bourgeoisie than by the fettered thought of those strata, which is filled with specific contents and bound to tangible matter. Its inadequacy for abstract economic thinking surely also underlies the employer's complaint about the indolence of many employees.

In exceptional cases correspondences do admittedly occur, lending credit to a preordained harmony. I know a cigarette salesman who represents his trade as perfectly as though he were born to it. He is what you might call a dashing fellow, he lives and lets live, he makes sparkling conversation, he has a way with women and opportunities. But the marvellous thing is that his manifold gifts are not just empty arabesques, as is usually the case with salesmen and representatives, but derive from a real basis and sit well on him. Nature herself is dashing

here: a demeanour normally indicating a person who lives only in
relations with other people derives here from plentiful resources.
According to his own account, he is received like a prince when he
drives up to see customers in his splendid company car. Since the
elegant car is just the right accessory for him, he likes to use it also for
excursions with ladies and other private purposes; a generosity which,
as he sees it, in return indirectly benefits the company, from which he
has never concealed these additional trips. (In the meantime, alas,
thanks to the advancing process of concentration in the cigarette
industry, car use has been rationed – so the ladies will be left out in the
cold.) The man is of modest origins and has his roots in the heart of
Berlin. Other people, endowed with his talents and income, see it as
their task in life to be gentlemen belonging to the upper class. He, on
the other hand, unaffected by the high life or the opportunities he
could no doubt exploit with the help of his friendly charm, sticks to his
employee union, to which he has already introduced many non-
unionized people. After conferences or local branch meetings, he often
repairs with male and female colleagues to coaching inns or semi-
proletarian bars, in which he is just as much at home as in the car. He
is well acquainted with landlords and piano-players and knows all about
the customers. The atmosphere soon grows lively, since neither women
nor men can seriously resist this mixture of native wit, irreverence and
feeling. His popularity reaches its zenith when he begins singing, in a
passable voice, from *La Traviata* and *Lohengrin*. Then everyday reality
vanishes and all those present, far beyond the circle of colleagues, revel
in the enjoyment of a more beautiful life.

Not often does the economy leave empty such a gap, in which a
person from a lower stratum who is something is permitted to be just as
he is. Many remain insecure throughout their lives, like that thoroughly
petite-bourgeoise female secretary of my acquaintance who tries to
feign a measure of experience by always inserting an English 'Well . . .'
into her conversation. She has taken this 'Well' from the linguistic
arsenal of the successful who get by effortlessly; but despite this crutch
she does not really make much progress, although she already has ten
jobs under her belt. An eventful life, but one that has no direction,
since in terms of substance it is warped by the demands of the modern
firm. Those without substance have an easier time. At least the girl can
still just keep up, while others have to exorcise their nature merely in
order to survive in one modest job. I once spent an evening with a
number of older employees, who in the daytime are engaged in average
commercial jobs. One is an accountant, a second a cashier – sober men,
normally quite unremarkable outside office life and the narrow domestic circle. That evening we attended a ball for widows in the

neighbourhood of Elsässerstrasse, the real Zille milieu,[5] with brass-band music, casual workers, cheap widows and whores. Beer was drunk and the men metamorphosed before my eyes. They were no longer repressed office employees, but real elemental forces breaking out of their cage and enjoying themselves in quite reckless ways. They told crude stories, dug up comic anecdotes, prowled about the room, brooded into their glasses, then went wild again. The impresario came over to the table, a rather doddery popular comedian who, when treated to a beer, held forth unbidden on his fate. He had known his heyday as a musical clown, and since then had evidently gone downhill little by little. But what was particularly noteworthy about the encounter was the fact that the accountant seemed like an old crony of the dancing master, like a thoroughly non-bourgeois character who had never seen the inside of an office at all. Why did he never make his way up to higher positions? Perhaps the indifference of a vagabond nature prevented his ascent, and now it is too late. There are a great many fantastical E. T. A. Hoffmann figures among employees of advanced years.[6] They have got stuck somewhere, performing unremittingly banal functions that are anything but uncanny. Yet it is as though these men were shrouded in an aura of horror. It emanates from the decayed powers that have found no outlet within the existing order.

The young people growing up in the broad strata between the proletariat and the bourgeoisie adapt themselves more or less easily to the firm. Many drift along unwittingly and join without ever suspecting that they really do not belong there.

I recall a girl whom her friends nickname 'Cricket'.[7] Cricket is a proletarian child who lives not far from Gesundbrunnen and works in the filing room of a factory. The magic of bourgeois life reaches her only in its meanest form, and she accepts unthinkingly all the blessings that trickle down from above. It is typical of her that, in a dancehall or suburban café, she cannot hear a piece of music without at once chirruping the appropriate popular hit. But it is not she who knows every hit, rather the hits know her, steal up behind her and gently lay her low. She is left in a state of total stupor. Some of her recent young female colleagues have greater powers of resistance. Though they do not really fight against temptations they cannot master anyway, they

5. Heinrich Zille (1858–1929) was a social caricaturist who portrayed Berlin proletarian life affectionately.
6. E. T. A. Hoffmann (1776–1822): German romantic novelist and composer, author of gothic tales of madness, grotesquerie and the supernatural. Offenbach's opera *Tales of Hoffmann* is based on three of his stories.
7. *Heimchen* (cricket) stands for *Heimchen am Herd* (Cricket on the Hearth – an allusion to the story by Charles Dickens), and means 'little housewife'.

seem for the time being to be surrounded by an invisible cocoon beneath which they move about unimperilled. You meet them in department stores, in lawyers' offices and in firms of every kind – unassuming creatures who live with their parents in the north or east and still have barely any idea where they are actually going. They are easy to cope with. At all events, several girls of this kind, trainees or already trained, have struck me as quite contented. Their experience in business is of a touching triviality. One tells me she cannot add up if a barrel-organ is playing outside. Her companion is delighted because she has recently been able to travel by taxi on the firm's business. And a third sometimes gets free tickets for the Luna Park and a variety show. They know, of course, that with their small income they would have to have a friend, if they possessed no relatives. But for now they have relatives, and the friend is usually a fiancé, with whom they camp out on Sundays in a tent. For want of money they almost never go to bars, and in general they are pretty respectable. You should just hear how Trude, a salesgirl in Moabit, dissociates herself from colleagues wearing make-up – whom, incidentally, the working-class buying public also holds in dislike; how she and her friend pass judgement on the girls of easy virtue who, of an evening, eat slap-up meals in male company at Kempinski's. So much the worse for those girls if they end up marrying people like themselves, say the immature young things, who themselves like to dream about the joy of being able some day to call themselves married women. Their ideal is petit bourgeois: an intended who displays commitment to the family and earns so much that they no longer need to work. The only thing they do not want is children. Inherited moral concepts, religious ideas, superstition and transmitted wisdom from humble parlours – all this is carried along and hurled anachronistically against the prevailing praxis of life. These undercurrents should not be forgotten. Where they are present, intractable struggles break out between individuals and their environment. For instance, the sexual freedom normal today causes young people considerable trouble, particularly among employees of the lowlier kind. They would like to express their own feelings; they defy the system that seeks to determine their being, and yet they are overwhelmed by the system. If they are dull and narrow-minded like a certain 21-year-old business employee I know, terrible deformations develop. This young man, who grew up on the fringes of the proletarian milieu, belongs to an employee union in which he is fanatically active. Since he yearns for spiritual interchange, and evidently finds few people of like mind even in the youth group of his organization, he has struck up a correspondence with a girl in the provinces who is also a union member. Now this private correspondence is conducted by him according to methods that would be worthy of the filing department of a large-scale enterprise.

The fact that the documents are filed chronologically in folders is to some extent still understandable. But, in addition, every meaningless picture postcard carries its incoming or outgoing stamp, and letters dispatched are preserved in the original shorthand copy. The insanity with which business principles here penetrate a field where they have no place would be an isolated exception, if in the letters a straitjacket were not applied to feelings as well. Let us call the recipient Käthe. Both address each other not by their first names, say, but as young colleagues. 'Dear young colleague', writes the nineteen-year-old girl. In this use of titles, some misplaced union collectivism has a wretched little field-day. If the latter's linguistic creativity flags, business German at once steps in to continue the muzzling. Käthe writes: 'I am sending you enclosed the programme for our parents' evening.' And at the end of one letter she puts on record: 'I look forward to your next communication.' But resistance to the business of life all round is so strong that it still stirs despite all the fetters. Again and again the question of sexual behaviour crops up. 'What position do we take now towards sexual intercourse in general?' asks Käthe. 'Should young people have such relations before marriage? I answer in the affirmative, on condition that the said people are mature and in *spiritual* harmony – i.e. not just physical attraction, but also spiritual understanding! Well, the latter is of course absent today in the majority of cases ... How can we remedy this? It is my view that the woman has a large area of responsibility here, since the man is not usually endowed with spirituality, but is formed only through association with good women.' Käthe, who incidentally is of Catholic origin, wants to be such a woman. 'I have reached the point today', one epistle runs, 'where I can trace back sexual misdemeanours, or rather those related to gender, to the whole personality – &, this is the essential thing here, for the sake of these people's good sides I can disregard their initial faults, and fight against my egoism, in order to eliminate or mitigate other people's bad sides through my good side and then, with combined forces, obtain from this community something creative for the great national community...' The letter-filer also maintains a platonic long-distance correspondence with another young female colleague, one who is not so enlightened, luminous and idealistic as Käthe, but can give only a quite confused account of her feelings. In a melancholic tone, whose naivety is moving, she complains about the disastrous superficiality with which sexual relations are commonly pursued. One of her girl friends has got involved with a man and seems to have become pregnant. She comments on this: 'Boys are willing to ruin girls, if they see how things are with them; it's mainly done in a drunken state, of course, so they can deny it afterwards. I admit it's often the girl's fault too of course, she can prevent it by keeping a clear head, and that's not the case, they abandon themselves to sensual pleasure, because they think: now he can't let me go any more, he has got to marry me; now I've got someone to provide for me, as the saying goes.' What floats on the surface is more careless, though – and if things go wrong they have it scraped out, as the saying goes.

The feeble resistance from below has no power over the normal everyday life of the mass of employees. Elements from the higher regions too flow into it, but they barely affect it, much less really change anything. In many offices the daughters of solid bourgeois families tap away; for them it is simply a matter of any old occupation to bring in pocket money. They may join in or they may keep to themselves – either way they leave things just as they are. From the main body of such higher bourgeois reinforcements, a type stands out that is quite frequently to be met with particularly in Berlin and that can best be described as salaried-bohemian: girls who come to the big city in search of adventure and roam like comets through the world of salaried employees. Their career is unpredictable and even the best astronomer cannot determine whether they will end up on the street or in the marriage bed. A perfect example of this genus is the nice manufacturer's daughter from western Germany who often resides in the Romanische Café. She likes it better there than with her family, from which she ran away one fine day, in her beret with the little point on top. Better too than in the big firm where she works at an adding machine for 150 Marks a month. What is one to do, if one wants to live, really live, and does not get the smallest allowance from home? To be sure, she wants to get herself a higher position and will do so; but office work for her is still always only the indispensable condition of the freedom she wants to enjoy. After closing time, at home in her furnished room, she first gulps down a strong coffee to freshen her up again, then it is off and away into the midst of life, to the students and artists with whom there is chatter and smoking and canoeing. More than that probably happens too. After a short while, she will disappear. But in the offices her colleagues remain.

# Refined informality

'The active personnel policy', the director responsible for personnel matters in a large banking institute explains to me, 'is a result of the greater economic difficulties – just as, in agriculture, intensive cultivation is now required in place of the former extensive kind.' Whether the implementation of this guiding principle has been successful in agriculture remains an open question. The effort of most big firms to form the mass of their employees into a community depending on the firm, and feeling at one with it, originates not least from their need to intensify as required. 'We look forward to the great organism being filled with life . . .' says the opening article in a certain giant enterprise's company newspaper, 'a wish that can be fulfilled only if these monthly issues are understood as expressions of a circle of people bound to a common endeavour.' And the house paper of one huge specialist shop extends to its staff on the front page the following New Year's greeting: 'We wish you a good 1929 and implore you, in the new year too, to continue to do your best in our dedicated working community for the success of our community work!' In order to enhance the community work, by the way, in the same number the house paper immediately supplements its end-of-year congratulations with moral lessons. 'Time is money!' it proclaims. 'And particularly so at the start of work each morning – so be punctual! Remember: the early bird catches the worm!'

Many employers have highly subjective notions of a community. The lady supervisors of one well-known department store address their subordinates as 'Child'. Perhaps this family atmosphere does perhaps lend wings to the children's enthusiasm, but it is not really very affecting, enforced as it is by checks that express only a limited confidence in its warmth. How far many of these checks would like to extend emerges from the guidelines recently drawn up by the organ of the Association of Retail and Department Stores. These recommend, among other things:

Staff exit by one particular door, wrapped purchases to be released there on prescribed buying days; in case of suspicion, and as a deterrent preventive measure, other luggage items, handbags, etc., to be checked. Watch out for any unnatural alteration in girth! Do not leave personal checking just to the porter: he may be an accessory to the disloyalty of employees. In the event of any unscheduled departure from the building, use extra vigilance! . . .

quoted from the GdA's *Gewerkschaftlichen Aufklärungsblätter*, no. 2, April 1929

The advice, whose excessive bluntness has fortunately incurred disapproval even among employers, is a compilation of well-tried recipes which proves at least that reliance is not always placed solely on the virtue of community. The latter is utterly disavowed by such provisions aimed at isolating the firm's employees. But isolation of the different categories of staff from one another is sought also because the firm's interest in the productive power of the community spirit intersects with its interest in weakening the influence of the employee unions. The separation between wage-workers and salaried employees still remains to be discussed in detail. For employees themselves the principle of individual remuneration is pitted against the method of pay agreements, which are regarded by the employers as an inconvenient collective will's intrusion into the natural laws of the free economy. But if everyone has to fend for himself like this, community is a sham.

More and more do large employers insist upon this sham, more and more do they come to realize that – in a period of collectivist arrangements – nothing would be more mistaken than to leave easily excited collective powers either to themselves or to the adversary. The attempt to attract them to their own side is not much helped by welfare institutions in the narrow sense. In a whole number of companies there exist provident and pension funds, holiday and marriage endowments, convalescent homes, etc. – generous, and assuredly also liberally administered, foundations that are supposed to provide a counterweight to income. They do keep individuals in a dependent state, to be sure, but they are unable to awaken the collective spirit. This is conjured up by other means, by arrangements that strive to confiscate the soul and guide everybody in a particular direction. Just as old, long-forgotten tunes emanate from the electrically powered organ, so do paternalistic life forms develop on the basis of the modern economy. Instead of working conditions being the fruit of proper human relations, rationalization engenders a neo-paternalism that seeks to manufacture such relations subsequently.

Not infrequently, a sense of humane obligation may extend beyond what is necessary. Many firms really do worry about the well-being of their staff and show them a regard that, despite its perhaps paternalist nature, must certainly be distinguished from those measures whose intention is to harness the mass soul. Since the latter finds fulfilment today mainly in sport, sports clubs are one of the most important instruments for its conquest. Berlin university professor W. His seems to be of a similar opinion, for he explains in a lecture that has, not inappropriately, been reprinted in the organ of the sports association of a certain large bank:

> The importance in life of the instincts cannot be overestimated. They are the steam that drives the machine. Repressing them means killing life. But as we can see they allow themselves to be directed, for better or for worse. A good society is one that understands how to direct the instincts so that they will ensure its survival and progress. Physical exercise and sport are among the right directions – so they deserve all support.

The lecture is naturally entitled: 'To Personality Through Sport'. If what is so repeatedly asserted in it were true, the world would be simply teeming with personalities. Perhaps it is on the way to that, for many big companies do not shrink even from considerable expenditure for sports purposes. They have created sports associations that are divided into as many sections as there are types of sport. Football, athletics, boxing, handball, rowing, gymnastics, hockey, swimming, tennis, cycling, jiu-jitsu – nothing is forgotten. Devotees of sport have sports rooms available within the building, and also their own sports grounds. As these usually lie far out, the sports union of one huge enterprise has had a bus bestowed upon it from some prominent source, in order to ferry its members to and fro. The bus may also be requested gratis for Sunday excursions with wives and children, whose destination is often the boathouse. Thus are sport and family fused. Another firm has engaged a special athletics coach for its staff. The associations are usually autonomous, but without therefore being removed from the overall supervision of the firms, which monitor their financial conduct and are represented within the groups by heads or delegates of the personnel department. Thanks to the high subsidies, members need pay only a small subscription, for which they could nowhere else gain admittance to such grand facilities for exercise. Training takes place, competitions are fought out. The Berlin Industrial Relay is famous. We find in a newspaper report on this year's public activities:

Thirty-one runners started off from the town hall, and raced down König-strasse and Unter den Linden. Here Dresdner Bank held the lead, but in Moabit it was caught and replaced by the Verkehrsgesellschaft. Then the picture changed once more, since several teams' swimmers were too weak. So Peek u. Cloppenburg came out of the water first, but was subsequently hard pressed by Siemens, Osram and Reichskreditgesellschaft, of whom Osram later emerged from the pack to take the lead.

The fact that the fighting troops bore the names of their firms is not the worst advertisement; and at the same time it increases the feeling of solidarity, which is also indirectly reinforced by orchestral and choral societies. For its further intensification, social evenings, summer festivals on a grand scale and collective steamer trips take place at company expense. Dionysian lust cements the bond.

Are these patriarchal events staged as 'company communities' [*Werks-gemeinschaften*], as recommended by DINTA? Set up in its day by west-German heavy industry, DINTA (Deutsches Institut für technische Arbeitsschulung [German Institute for Technical Training at Work]), as is well known, works by all possible methods and means to wean employees away from the class struggle, pacify them within the present economic system, and bring them into the closest alliance with the firm. Yellow company associations for employees are undoubtedly the distinct wish of many employers.[8] Far removed, on the other hand, from such inclinations towards economic peace is, for instance, the progressive personnel boss of a large firm who assures me that he absolutely rejects company communities. ('One can't accomplish anything against the workers any more', he tells me during our conversation, 'and hardly anything without them.') 'Well, send your members in, then', he told the union representatives when a sports association was being estab-lished and they were afraid he too might now be taking a yellow line. Quite logically, like the other directors he declined to take over the honorary presidency and explained from the outset that he was not demanding any 'good attitude'. But he removes obstacles that prevent such an attitude from emerging when he requests the exclusion of politics from the sports field and warns the team always to bear in mind that it belongs to the firm. In one propaganda leaflet devoted to the company's welfare activities you may read, then, how the sports groups strive to give of their best for the firm's colours. So even if an authentic company community is not striven for, at least the energy sources of the collective are supposed to gush forth for the benefit of the firm. Between the extremes, there are transitional steps. One works-council

8. Yellow was a colour symbolizing class collaboration in the slang of the 1920s' socialist movement.

chairman, for instance, tells me how in his firm they either circumvent the election of any oppositionist as a committee member of the sports association, or they make the individual aware of his false position. So far as the conscious motives inciting employers to foster sporting activity are concerned, their disinterested liking for employees in peak condition combines with certain practical considerations that are not hard to fathom.[9] One is particularly pleased that sport revives a sense of comradeship. Another calculates that money spent on the health of the staff will perhaps flow back in. 'We want people to keep suitable company too', he goes on candidly, 'and friends who are colleagues are always best.' A questionable assertion. The pressure for inbreeding is due, unless I am very much mistaken, to certain trade unions that are apparently unsuitable company. Whether or not we are dealing with company communities, at all events sports associations represent an important part of the firm. Young people, union members as well as the non-unionized, are subjected to a gentle moral pressure that is supposed to induce them to join. Sporting talents are sometimes even decisive for getting a job, and it is presumably no exaggeration when one deputy assures me that an outstanding left 'winger' will more easily wing his way into any vacant position – at least in the lower echelons, where there are not so many other distinguishing features. Correspondingly, to judge by the experiences of one elderly works-council member, vassals owing their position to sport are marked out within the firm by greater goodwill. Whoever is an important athlete will generally get leave for competitions without any difficulty. And if redundancies are planned, a blind eye tends to be turned towards sporting colleagues. How do those people fare who resist temptation and, for some reason, do not allow themselves to be recruited? One intelligent younger technician tells me he would gain in prestige with his boss if he were ready to swim, row or run with his colleagues. In order to escape the not always harmless consequences of a lesser prestige, some people prefer to renounce their independence. I know of one departmental head who has surrendered to the sports business of business sports for the simple reason that he does not want to arouse his boss's suspicion that he may be denying recognition to such expressions of community. The value placed on them by the higher authorities shows that they serve to enhance the company's power. To be precise, sports associations are like outposts intended to conquer the still vacant territory of the employees' souls. Indeed they often carry out a thorough process of colonization there. The soil is admittedly still fertile from pre-war

9. The concept of *interesseloses Wohlgefallen*, or disinterested liking, is borrowed from Kant (*Critique of Judgement*).

times, and the good attitude will quite frequently burgeon of its own accord. There are probably plenty of people who feign it for the sake of their own advancement: so-called 'blood oranges' – yellow on the outside, red within. You flatter the bosses in the sports groups; you bathe in the radiance of the merciful sun that rises over employees on festive occasions, in the shape of some great patron or other. 'No stiff, solemn ball characterized by grave dignity and respectable boredom', enthuses the diarist of one works newspaper over an event at the rowing club attached to the firm,

> but a family party ... in the setting of the rowing club ... all a colourful medley, many leading gentlemen from our establishment with their ladies ... and, as a special honour for us, the chairman of the board of directors, Privy Counsellor X, who nodded affably to the dancing couples and appeared to feel entirely at his ease. No reserve, no separation, a purely human get-together for the pride and pleasure of the coming generation. 'Refined informality' was the watchword of the evening.

Hard to decide which is more pitiable: the confusion of joviality with a purely human get-together, or the over-zealous triumph at the fall of barriers. Probably not everyone has the good fortune to feel at ease in such circumstances.

In employee-union circles, the conviction prevails that company sports associations do not primarily serve the purpose of physical training, but are intended to distract from trade-union interests. Various works-council members tell me of their experiences. Young people especially, says one, easily fall for a magic that is as cheap as it is marvellous; while another maintains that employees blessed from on high with the pleasures of sport gradually slip away from the staff councils. The contest with the neo-paternalist structures for the time being occurs in the form of fierce propaganda skirmishes. 'They Are After our Souls!' runs the title of a piece by Fritz Fricke (put out by the publishing house of the General Confederation of German Trade Unions), in which among other things he argues: 'Are we perhaps to recognize the will to community from the fact that, in a growing crisis, the employer first seeks to protect the interest on his capital by depressing wages, lengthening working hours and sacking workers?' And he draws the succinct conclusion: 'An integration of interests between employer and worker is quite impossible, so long as the economy is organized exclusively on a private-enterprise ... basis.' The theoretical rejection is matched by practical conduct. Even if some officials do not really believe in the seductive power of company events, worried souls still warn against sporting activity even in mixed enterprises; and alternative sports associations of the employee unions seek to direct the steam of the instincts into their own machine. Thoughts collide, objects exist close together in space.[10] A ghostly battle on the sports fields for the souls of the masses. All the more relentless because dreams are at stake.

10. Allusion to Schiller's 'Death of Wallenstein', Act II, Scene 2: 'Thoughts can exist so easily together/But objects in a space will soon collide.' See *Plays II*, translated by Jeanne Willson, Continuum, New York 1991, p. 152.

# Among neighbours

'A uniform stratum of employees is in the process of formation. The grouping of the population according to class viewpoint has made big advances since the pre-war period.' What Emil Lederer and Jakob Marschak maintain in their excellent study 'The New Middle Class' (*Grundriss der Sozialökonomik*, Section IX, Part 1), which in 1926 directed attention for the first time to the altered condition of salaried employees, Lederer himself has just recently had to qualify anew. 'Even if the capitalist intermediate strata today already share the destiny of the proletariat', he writes in his study 'The Restructuring of the Proletariat' (included in the August 1929 issue of the *Neue Rundschau*), 'the majority of them have nevertheless not yet abandoned their bourgeois ideology.' His judgement is shared by Richard Woldt, who in a treatise on German trade unions in the post-war period (incorporated in the collective work *Strukturwandlungen der Deutschen Volkswirtschaft* ['Structural changes in the German national economy']) characterizes as follows the attitude of the middle strata in decline: 'A certain professional ideology still stands in a relationship of tension with the actual facts.' Large sections of the population today do indeed base their bourgeois existence, which is no longer bourgeois at all, on monthly salaries, so-called intellectual labour and a few other similarly trivial characteristics. In total harmony with the experience articulated by Marx: that the superstructure adapts itself only slowly to the development of the base provoked by the forces of production. The position of these strata in the economic process has changed, their middle-class conception of life has remained. They nurture a false consciousness. They would like to defend differences, the acknowledgement of which obscures their situation; they devote themselves to an individualism that would be justified only if they could still shape their fate as individuals. Even where they struggle as wage-earners in and with the unions for better conditions of existence, their real existence is often conditioned by the better one which they once had. A vanished bourgeois way of life haunts them. Perhaps it contains forces with a legitimate demand to endure. But they survive today only inertly, without getting involved in a dialectic with the prevailing conditions, and so themselves undermine the legitimacy of their continued existence.

The aforementioned study 'The New Middle Class' notes that the boundary between civil servants and private employees is harder and harder to establish; that the salaried employee is indeed drawing closer to civil-servant status and the civil servant to salaried-employee status. Reichstag Deputy Aufhäuser expresses himself in the same vein in an article in *Der Beamte* ['The civil servant'], the new quarterly published by A. Falkenberg: 'The distinction between civil servants and salaried employees is provided today only by the different conditions of employment in terms of labour law.' Another deputy expresses himself even more drastically in conversation with me. 'Civil servants are workers just as employees are', he says, 'because they have nothing to sell but their labour-power.' A very candid generalization, which shows the extent to which economic thought has already conquered positions formerly outside its control. Does the common oppression lead to the formation of a common front? It is perhaps understandable that most civil servants are haunted by the old authoritarian state, in which they were the authority. Since man does not live by bread alone, they strive when dealing with lesser administrative employees to maintain a prestige that they no longer incontestably possess. Less so in local authorities or social departments than in the national or state civil service, the nature reserve of proper sovereign functions. Here as everywhere employees pour in and, even if at first they are not promoted to qualified posts (except, say, in employment offices), the influx is still quite capable of stripping civil-service power of its mystery. The salaried employee: for civil servants, this is a person from the very same public that only recently had to wait modestly in front of the window behind which they themselves sat enthroned in majesty. Their entire aura is dispelled if the interlopers carry out the same work as they do. So not just self-importance, but fear of competition too, bids them defend their sovereign territory. For the time being, at all events, their aura is not really all that badly damaged; thanks partly to the Social-Democratic Party, which is afraid of being too brave where civil servants are concerned, as one of its prominent officials assures me. He is convinced that this explains a certain half-heartedness on the part of civil servants organized in the Free trade unions, who have been intimidated not least by the cut-back in government employment. 'Leave me alone' is their watchword. 'I have to take care of my family.' It is only recently, in his judgement, that the political activity of those in unions has begun to stir again.

The distinct mania in bourgeois Germany to raise oneself from the
crowd by means of some rank, be it only an imaginary one, hampers
solidarity among salaried employees themselves. They are dependent
on each other and would like to separate from one another. One might
take pleasure in the endless varieties, if these were encompassed within
a unitary conviction. But they impede the consciousness of unity rather
than take root in it. Even the lowest groups of employees behave as
though they were worlds apart. One Berlin newspaper recently published a story, the point of which was that a female dispatch clerk in a
department store fancies herself immeasurably superior to her colleague, who merely has to ensure the link between warehouse and
goods-collection point. Similarly, women with office jobs in the store
are commonly more respected than the salesgirls, indeed they enjoy an
esteem roughly expressed by the honorary title bestowed upon them of
'Princess'. The unsuspecting layman observing these immense differences of importance feels as though a new cosmos full of abysses and
peaks were coming into view beneath his microscope lens. A chasm of
impressive depth yawns likewise between, for example, technical and
commercial employees in industry. The latter, according to the report
of one victim, treat the former with disdain and like to make them wait
like unimportant customers; while the former, on the other hand,
nurture the prejudice that their work alone should be seen as productive. The idea that the bank official is the lord of creation among
employees is a widely held article of faith, at least among bank officials.
It has been handed down since the earliest days of the profession, it is
evidently connected with the intimate involvement with money, and it
gains a kind of external confirmation from lavish banking palaces in
the Renaissance style. Thus do cathedrals increase the piety from which
they have arisen. As the works-council chairman of one large bank
explains to me, the huge retrenchment has merely shaken the heredi-
tary master caste's sense of rank, but in no way eliminated it. His
comment is substantiated marvellously by the information of one
member of the Deutsche Bankbeamtenverein: to his observation that
the horizon of bank employees today is unfortunately narrower than it
used to be, the official in question appends the comforting postscript
that they nevertheless generally still possess more education than
related categories of employee. Asserting their sovereignty is supposed
to sustain their impaired self-confidence.


All these contradistinctions shrivel to mere nuances in comparison with
that between workers and salaried employees. This is felt as a class
distinction, although on the decisive count and for any length of time

it is no longer one. Not just the employees, who should know better, cling to it, but even more do the workers, who have apparently failed to notice its waning. At least this is the judgement of one well-informed trade-union official, who traces the common proletarian view – that salaried employees still play the same role within the bourgeoisie as before – to the outsider situation of the workers, which blinds them to the decay of the bourgeois world. How convinced they still are of the delights of the employee's existence emerges unambiguously from the fact that fewer employees were registered in the 1925 census of firms than in the simultaneous census of jobs, in which many workers designated themselves of their own accord as employees. What they are not, their offspring are supposed to become – and they picture them making a rapid ascent. At all events, parent workers among the clients of one career adviser for a Free employee union always remonstrate with him to the effect that they want their children one day to have better, easier and 'cleaner' work than they perform themselves. The children are usually no less eager to look smart and lead a lively existence. Thus a large proportion of the people comprising the Zentralverband der Angestellten are actually of proletarian origin. Sometimes the circle closes and as a consequence of retrenchment they once more return, the richer for a few experiences, to their fathers' station. Salaried employees understandably endeavour not to shatter the workers' belief in their celestial nature. However sure it may be that a clerk in industry is more different from a chief clerk in business than he is from a skilled worker, it is just as sure that he considers himself the chief clerk's colleague. Under the heading 'What questionnaires reveal', one of this year's issues of the GdA journal reports: 'Thus there are frequently recurring complaints from salaried employees, young and old alike, that workers in the firm earn more than an employee does . . .' That is certainly absurd, and it can just be considered fortunate that many of them doubtless salve their wounded self-esteem by following the example of the bank official who tells me how membership of the proletariat, in his opinion, does not depend on income alone. In accordance with this statement, numerous salaried employees are averse to any closer intercourse with the comrades: the main exception being technical employees, who thanks to their activity in the firm have sufficient opportunity to learn respect for the workers. I know, for instance, that the salaried employees of one well-known firm recently refused to allow the industrial workers employed in the company to attend a party they had organized; whereas the latter, by contrast, have never been so exclusive. Only the intervention of the paternalistic boss succeeded in tempering the megalomania of his higher-ranking vassals. In particular girls who have got salaried jobs usually think they are too good for workers. Or else their parents have higher ambitions for them. One young salesgirl told me about her friendship with a skilled metalworker, who changed his job under pressure from her father. The father is a court usher, no less, and will consequently tolerate no worker in the family. Her beloved now has to content himself with the lowly position of bank messenger – but in return he has progressed to fiancé.

To divide those whose alliance might threaten them has been an axiom from time immemorial for the wielders of power. In obedience to it some employers more or less consciously separate people who often already, of their own accord, do not wish to remain together. Thus from one, admittedly thoroughly reactionary, industrial plant it is reported to me that the management strives as far as possible to prevent any direct contact between salaried staff and workers. Typically, in this respect, an acting commercial director took one of his subordinates to task not long ago for holding a conversation with a worker in the yard. In another large industrial company, a relationship as between colleagues grew up between groups of salaried staff and workers, and was sealed by the custom of so-called 'holiday rounds': i.e. the lucky ones with leave due would always stand their colleagues and comrades a round of beer before going on holiday. At some point a departmental manager temporarily in charge learnt of this conspiracy: he gave the guilty workshop clerk his notice on the spot. Such tyrants of lesser rank are even termed 'cock robins' in the company slang.[11] The notice could not be rescinded, but after a protest by the works council the dismissed man was at least awarded some compensation. Senior managers are often more broad-minded than the multitude of those who would like to win their favour. A qualified engineer informs me how, one day during a workers' strike, one of his directors conversed with two pickets in a conspicuous place. The event took on as it were historic significance, since from that moment on the salaried staff too condescended to greet the workers, of whom they had previously taken no notice.

*Divide et impera* has found its more or less explicit ideologues. Thus J. Winschuh comes close to defending the principle when, for instance, he explains in his book *Praktische Werkspolitik* published in 1921: 'Precisely association ... within the salariat has the virtue of uniting civil servants and imparting ... to them what they need in order to make them gradually into a utilizable factor of industrial labour policy: corporate pride, cohesion, a self-seclusion against influences dragging

11. *Zaunkönig*, literally king of the hedge, actually means 'wren'.

them down. ...' A lapse that may be attributed to impressions in the post-war years; for Fricke himself, who quotes the passage polemically in his earlier-mentioned study 'They Are After our Souls!', acknowledges that Winschuh has by now changed his views in many respects in favour of the trade unions. On Fricke's side and yet not on his side fights Dr Alfred Striemer, who likewise rejects a policy of separation between different categories of wage-earner. Striemer is today managing editor of the *Borsig-Zeitung*,[12] and has recently raised the question in his paper: 'Why are there workers and salaried employees?' More innocent students of ideology may be astonished to encounter his answers, especially in such a context. He disputes the validity of the opinion 'that the separation of workers and salaried employees above all serves capitalist interests, since such a separation facilitates control over the workers in general'. He dismisses the separatist yearnings of salaried employees with the words: 'The formation of a salaried-employee stratum in today's shape, brought about solely by modes of remuneration and notice, can in no way be described as right, since it socially divides millions of people in the wrong place, since the great mass of salaried employees are not leaders.' Do wolves dwell with lambs? Has Paradise come on earth? Simply by invoking the idea Striemer rejects it. For, in the very same breath as he calls for peace, he exposes the existing trade unions and brands them quite blatantly as trouble-makers. 'Due to the fact that the trade unions strive individually to influence the organism of the company or the economy', he writes in another essay in the same volume,

> they operate like 'foreign bodies' affecting more or less severely the vital interests of other parts of the organism! The particularistic attitude of the individual ... groups must give way to an attitude of solidarity vis-à-vis the individual company and the economy, one concerned with the whole – with workers and salaried staff of all kinds.

Perhaps it is not superfluous to mention that Striemer was once expelled from the Free trade unions for anti-union conduct. One is tempted to ask what lies behind his fine-sounding demand, and whether it does not involve him in skipping all too rashly over reality. At all events, it seems suspicious that he chooses to make the multiplicity of trade unions responsible for the disunity of their members, rather than other economic and social forces. De facto, through the way in which he sings the praises of solidarity, he certainly operates no differently

12. Borsig was a giant machine-building combine, founded by August Borsig in the first half of the nineteenth century, which gave its name to an entire district of Berlin; the *Borsig-Zeitung* was its company journal.

from those who naively endeavour to deepen the opposition between wage-earners by weakening the influence of trade unions; his idealistic construction is merely harder to see through than the pure calculation that bases itself on existing relations.

Even if salaried-employee organizations unanimously champion the material interests of the employed, they still seek to resolve in different ways the tension between the real living conditions of salaried employees and their ideology. They separate out and elevate into trends what, in individual employees, often exists all jumbled together in inchoate confusion. The extreme advocate of middle-class behaviour is the Deutschnationale Handlungsgehilfen-Verband, along with its related organizations. It is not bothered by the fact that its ideological stance comes more or less continually into conflict both with economic conditions in general and with its own operations in the field of wage negotiations; for the intermediate layers are a sufficient mass quickly to forget inconsistencies over the gratification of their instincts. One of its officials explains to me pointblank that the union assents to the term 'new middle class' and is keen on fostering class awareness. 'Will you be able to instil it even into people working at machines?' I ask him. 'Those people don't come into consideration at all for us.' In fact, the union regards itself as a kind of guild, which makes a selection from the various categories of employee with the aim of uniting only the elite. The rest, in this official's opinion, are basically rubbish. The bourgeois worldview can scarcely be more harshly and nakedly portrayed. The dustmen who collect the rubbish are for the most part in the Free trade unions; not to speak here of the Gewerkschaftsbund der Angestellten, which ideologically would like to create a balance between right and left and embodies, as it were, the middle stratum of the middle stratum. In accordance with their whole approach, the Free employee unions want the abolition of any traditional corporate pride, which keeps the majority of its upholders from any knowledge of their present position and is likely to frustrate their organizational alliance with the working class. Thus the Zentralverband der Angestellten, for example, especially in youth groups strives to form closer relations between its members and the proletariat. Many members of the unions organized in the Afa-Bund already originate from proletarian circles, of course, so they mostly know by birth what their social position is. As far as the rest – those who do not spring from the proletariat – are concerned, experienced officials make quite modest assessments regarding the possibility of their spiritual recomposition. It remains to be shown that they do not bear the sole blame for this failure.

# Shelter for the homeless

The average worker, upon whom so many lowly salaried employees like to look down, often enjoys not merely a material but also an existential superiority over them. His life as a class-conscious proletarian is roofed over with vulgar-Marxist concepts that do at least tell him what his intended role is. Admittedly the whole roof is nowadays riddled with holes.

The mass of salaried employees differ from the worker proletariat in that they are spiritually homeless. For the time being they cannot find their way to their comrades, and the house of bourgeois ideas and feelings in which they used to live has collapsed, its foundations eroded by economic development. They are living at present without a doctrine to look up at or a goal they might ascertain. So they live in fear of looking up and asking their way to the destination.

Nothing is more characteristic of this life, which only in a restricted sense can be called a life, than its view of higher things. Not as substance but as glamour. Yielded not through concentration, but in distraction. 'Why do people spend so much time in bars?' asks one employee I know. 'Probably because things are so miserable at home and they want to get a bit of glamour.' 'Home', by the way, should be taken to mean not just a lodging, but an everyday existence outlined by the advertisements in magazines for employees. These mainly concern: pens; Kohinoor pencils; haemorrhoids; hair loss; beds; crêpe soles; white teeth; rejuvenation elixirs; selling coffee to friends; dictaphones; writer's cramp; trembling, especially in the presence of others; quality pianos on weekly instalments; and so on. A shorthand-typist prone to reflection expresses herself in similar vein to the aforementioned employee: 'The girls mainly come from a modest milieu and are attracted by the glamour.' Then she gives an extremely odd reason for the fact that the girls generally avoid serious conversations. 'Serious conversations', she said, 'only distract and divert you from surroundings that you'd like to enjoy.' If distracting effects are ascribed to serious talk, distraction must be a deadly serious matter.


Things could be different. From results he obtained by investigating the household budget of salaried employees (as elaborated in his study *Die Lebenshaltung der Angestellten* ['The standard of living of salaried employees'], Freier Volksverlag, Berlin 1928), the Afa-Bund's economic policy adviser Otto Suhr draws the conclusion that employees do indeed devote less money to food than the average worker, but they rate so-called cultural needs more highly. The employee, according to Suhr, spends more on cultural requirements than on lodging (inclusive of heating and lighting), clothes and laundry combined. Along with health, transport, gifts, donations, etc., the category of 'cultural needs' covers, among other things, tobacco products, restaurants, and intellectual or social events. And society consciously – or even more, no doubt, unconsciously – sees to it that this demand for cultural needs does not lead to reflection on the roots of real culture, hence to criticism of the conditions underpinning its own power. Society does not stop the urge to live amid glamour and distraction, but encourages it wherever and however it can. As remains to be shown, society by no means drives the system of its own life to the decisive point, but on the contrary avoids decision and prefers the charms of life to its reality. Society too is dependent upon diversions. Since it sets the tone, it finds it all the easier to maintain employees in the belief that a life of distraction is at the same time a higher one. It posits itself as what is higher and, if the bulk of its dependants take it as a model, they are already almost where it wants them to be. The siren songs of which it is capable are demonstrated by the following excerpt from the department-store publicity brochure repeatedly cited above, which belongs in a model collection of classic ideologies:

> One further influence is worthy of mention, which derives from the layout and furnishing of the store. Many of the employees are from quite modest backgrounds. Perhaps their homes consist of cramped, poorly lit rooms; perhaps the people with whom they come into contact in their private lives are not very educated. In the store, however, the employees for the most part spend their time in cheerful rooms flooded with light. Contact with refined and well-educated customers is a constant source of fresh stimuli. The often quite awkward and self-conscious girl trainees more quickly accustom themselves to good behaviour and manners, they take care about their speech and also their appearance. The varied nature of their work broadens the sphere of their knowledge and improves their education. This facilitates their ascent to higher social strata.

If we leave aside the customers' education and the improvement – as may be done with a clear conscience – we are left with the cheerful rooms flooded with light and the higher social strata. The beneficent influence exercised by the flood of light, not just upon the urge to buy but also upon the staff, might at most consist in the staff being sufficiently duped to put up with their mean, poorly lit homes. The light blinds more than it illuminates – and perhaps the abundance of light pouring out lately over our large towns serves not least to increase the darkness. But do the higher strata not beckon? As it has turned out, they beckon from afar without commitment. The glamour they provide is indeed supposed to bind the mass of employees to society – but to raise them only just so far that they will remain more certainly in their appointed place. Instructive in this connection is a 'Ramble through fifteen account-books' that was published not long ago in *Uhu*. A few of the headings run: 'How come the Müllers can afford a sailing-boat?'; 'How come the Schulzes can pay 10 Marks for board and lodging on their summer holiday?'; 'However do the Wagners manage to go in for such expensive clothes?' Well, they simply can. Herr Schulze explains that his old lady is good at economizing, and Frau Wagner reports that her husband presses his own trousers. 'That's how you keep up appearances', she adds philosophically. Let us hope the trousers are not too shiny. In the same issue of the *Borsig-Zeitung* containing the essay by Dr Striemer mentioned in the previous chapter, an accountant answers the question of why there is a gulf between workers and salaried staff: 'It is mainly because everybody wants to appear more than he is.' Although many of the pleasures cut down on are undoubtedly real, the deeper moral of the *Uhu* expedition is obviously to inculcate in the so-called middle class the conviction that even with a modest income they can maintain the appearance of belonging to bourgeois society, so they have every reason to be content as the middle class. The fact that a chief clerk and a senior civil servant are mixed in with those questioned merely increases the middle-class dignity of the manager's secretary or minor civil servant likewise explored.

Encounters between employees and their superior models happen in the most marvellously natural way. Often the unintentional whiff of social life is sufficient to arouse slumbering forces. Such easy excitability is testified to, among other things, by the observation of a clerk from industry: if, in any department of his firm, even just a couple of employees had to come into contact with customers, the elegant demeanour of these outposts would at once begin to rub off on the rest of the staff. What is more, at every step imperceptible signals give a direction to yearning. Thus, in the window of one large department store, mannequin dolls strut about in cheap ready-made clothes among fancy orchids; in the Luna Park, meanwhile, an auto-racing track gives lowly salary-earners the pleasure of feeling like amateur motorists. Small effects, big causes.

For the masses, the delicate language of signs does not suffice. So where they flock together, as in Berlin, special shelters for the homeless are erected. Shelters in the literal sense are those gigantic taverns in which, as one garrulous fellow once put it in a Berlin evening paper, 'for not much money you can get a breath of the wide world'. The Haus Vaterland intended mainly for visitors from the provinces; the Resi (Residenz-Kasino), likewise catering for people on higher salaries; the Moka-Efti-Unternehmen – they and their like have been summoned forth by an unerring instinct, in order to calm a metropolitan population's hunger for glamour and distraction. 'Out of the business of work into the business of entertainment' is their unspoken motto. Not all categories of employee, incidentally, fall victim in equal measure to the spell of pervasive entertainment. One Reichstag deputy with a knowledge of the subject claims there is a very clear distinction between technicians and those employed, say, in the clothes trade. The former, according to the view he has expressed in conversation, generally tend to be loners, a bit old-fashioned and not really interested in making a fashionable impression. On the other hand, buyers and sales staff in the clothes trade – and doubtless in luxury shops too – have the understandable inclination to treat themselves to the elegance they constantly purvey, and they also like to idle away their nights for the sake of contact with customers. 'There exists a close connection', the deputy explains, 'between employees in the clothes trade and cabaret performers'. Both indeed have in common the fact that they work directly among the public, whereas technicians fashion their unsociable matter with their backs to the public. Entirely fitting, then, that the millionth visitor to the Haus Vaterland was precisely a buyer from a New York department store. For his services he received a silver cup. The fact that these 'pleasure barracks' began only recently to exercise their powers of attraction is anything but accidental. Replacing the countless dramshops of the inflation years, they were spawned as soon as the economy had been stabilized. At the same moment at which firms are rationalized, these establishments rationalize the pleasures of the salary-earning armies. My question as to why they treat the masses as a mere mass is met by one salaried employee with the bitter reply: 'Because people's lives are bled far too dry for them to have the least idea what to do with themselves.' No matter whether this is the case or no: in the establishments in question, the masses are their own guests; and, what is more, not just from any consideration for the commercial needs of the employer, but also for the sake of their own unavowed impotence. People warm each other, people console each other for the fact that they can no longer escape from the herd. Being part of it is made easier by the palatial surroundings. These are particularly plush in the Haus Vaterland, which embodies most completely the type roughly adhered to also in picture palaces and the establishments of the lower inter-mediate strata. Its nucleus is formed by a kind of immense hotel lobby, across whose carpets even the Adlon's guests would be able to walk without feeling demeaned.[13] Since only the most modern is good enough for our masses, this exaggerates the *neue Sachlichkeit* style.[14] The mystery of *die neue Sachlichkeit* could not be more conclusively exposed than here. From behind the pseudo-austerity of the lobby architecture, Grinzing grins out.[15] Just one step down and you are lapped in the most luxuriant sentimentality. But this is what characterizes *die neue Sach-lichkeit* in general, that it is a façade concealing nothing; that it does not derive from profundity, but simulates it. Like denial of old age, it arises from dread of confronting death. The room in which the new vintage is sampled presents a splendid view of Vienna by night. The Stephans-turm stands out faintly against the star-spangled sky, and an electric tram lit from within glides across the Danube Bridge. In other rooms adjoining the *neue Sachlichkeit* the Rhine flows past, the Golden Horn glows, lovely Spain extends far away in the south. All the more unnecessary to describe the sights, in that no word can be added to, or removed from, the matchless claims of the Haus Vaterland prospectus. This, for instance, is what it says about the Löwenbräu Bar: 'Bavarian landscape: Zugspitze with Eibsee – alpenglow – entry and dance of the Bavarian *Schuhplattler* lads';[16] and about the Wild West Bar: 'Prairie landscapes near the Great Lakes – Arizona – ranch – dancing – cowboy songs and dances – Negro and cowboy jazz band – well sprung dance-floor.' The Vaterland encompasses the entire globe. The fact that nineteenth-century panoramas are coming back into such high regard in all these establishments is related to the monotony in the sphere of work. The more monotony holds sway over the working day, the further

13. The Hotel Adlon: one of the most luxurious Berlin hotels in the early years of this century, recently restored.
14. *Die neue Sachlichkeit*: 'New Objectivity' – or 'New Sobriety', as the Weimar cultural critic and historian John Willett prefers. This was an aesthetic movement taking its name from a 1925 exhibition of pictures of 'tangible reality' put on in Mannheim by the gallery owner G. F. Hartlaub. Influencing a wide range of arts, it was consciously counterposed to expressionism.
15. Grinzing is a Viennese suburb associated with schmaltzy music and romantic nights out.
16. *Schuhplattler*: folk dance involving slapping of the thighs and shoe-soles.

away you must be transported once work ends – assuming that attention is to be diverted from the process of production in the background. The true counterstroke against the office machine, however, is the world vibrant with colour. The world not as it is, but as it appears in popular hits. A world every last corner of which is cleansed, as though with a vacuum cleaner, of the dust of everyday existence.

The geography of these shelters is born of the popular hit. Although this has but a vague knowledge of places, the panoramas are for the most part accurately executed: a pedantry that is not superfluous, since in the age of travel a holiday even on union pay allows many landscapes to be checked on the spot. Admittedly, what is depicted on the soffits is not so much real faraway places as imaginary fairy-tale scenes, in which illusions have become living figures. The sojourn between these walls, which signify the world, may be defined as a company outing to paradise for employees. The furnishing of the Moka-Efti-Lokal, whose spatial excesses are scarcely outdone by those of the Haus Vaterland, corresponds to this exactly. A moving staircase, whose functions presumably include symbolizing the easy ascent to the higher social strata, conveys ever new crowds from the street directly to the Orient, denoted by columns and harem gratings. The fantasy palace, by the way, resembles a dream image also in that it is not very solidly constructed; rather than on a firm subsoil of capital, it arises on short-term English credit. Up here you do not sit, you travel. 'Do not lean out!' is written upon the train window through which you gaze at nothing but sunny picture-postcard landscapes. In actual fact they are wall panels, and the realistically copied corridor of an international sleeper train is nothing more than a long, narrow passage connecting two Mohammedan halls with one another. The floods of light invoked in the department-store publicity brochure contribute everywhere to the ensemble. In the Resi they are dispatched through the room in myriad hues and play over the Heidelberg Castle depicted there with a wealth of colour that the setting sun would never manage. They are so much part of these establishments' defining features that you cannot help thinking that, during the day, the establishments are not there at all. Evening after evening they arise anew. But the real power of light is its presence. It alienates the masses from their habitual flesh, casts over them a costume that transforms them. Through its mysterious force glamour becomes substance, distraction stupor. If the waiter switches it off, though, the eight-hour day shines in again.


All events relating to the unorganized salaried masses, and equally all movements of these masses themselves, are today of an ambivalent nature. Inherent in them is a secondary significance that often distances them from their original determination. Under pressure from the prevailing society they become, in a metaphorical sense, shelters for the homeless. Apart from their primary purpose, they acquire the further one of binding employees by enchantment to the place the ruling stratum desires, and diverting them from critical questions – for which they anyway feel little inclination. So far as contemporary film production is concerned, I have demonstrated in two essays published in the *Frankfurter Zeitung* – 'The Little Shopgirls Go to the Movies' and 'Contemporary Film and its Audience'[17] – that almost all the industry's products serve to legitimize the existing order, by concealing both its abuses and its foundations. They, too, drug the populace with the pseudo-glamour of counterfeit social heights, just as hypnotists use glittering objects to put their subjects to sleep. The same applies to the illustrated papers and the majority of magazines. A closer analysis would presumably show that the image-motifs constantly recurring in them like magical incantations are intended to cast certain contents once and for all into the abyss of imageless oblivion: those contents that are not embraced by the construction of our social existence, but that bracket this existence itself. The flight of images is a flight from revolution and from death.

If the magic of images assails the masses from without, then sport – indeed the whole culture of the body, which has led also to the custom of the weekend – is a primary form of their existence. The systematic training of the body no doubt fulfils the mission of producing a vitally necessary counterweight to the increased demands of the modern economy. The question, however, is whether the contemporary sports industry is concerned only with this admittedly indispensable training. Or whether sport is not ultimately assigned so eminent a place in the hierarchy of collective values today because it offers the masses a welcome opportunity for distraction – which they exploit to the full. For distraction, in the most crucial sense of the word, and also for glamour. Numerous people who otherwise would remain faceless soldiers in the employee army can win prestige as sporting celebrities. It is the masses themselves who throng to the sports grounds. If a number of big firms did not think they needed their own company sports associations, society as a whole would hardly still have to whip up enthusiasm for sport in order to preserve itself. One discerning manufacturer complains in conversation with me that sport monopolizes the interest of young

17. *The Mass Ornament. Weimar Essays*, translated and edited by Thomas Levin, Harvard University Press, Cambridge Mass. and London 1995, pp. 291–304 and 307–20.

people. 'If I remind them of work, they say you live only once', he adds. But the natural life that you live only once can be so desirable only if it evades knowledge; only if it seeks to escape awareness of the context in which it exists. As it swirls up it also loses its sparkle; and where you live only once, you live little. On this one point Lederer's previously quoted essay 'The Restructuring of the Proletariat' certainly errs. Lederer writes:

> The spread of sport makes people confident, resolves complexes or prevents them from arising in the first place, and establishes a preliminary organization of the masses to which the individual actively adapts himself and in which he obtains a function, one in which all are united by a free and common will. . . . Is one really to assume that people who know all about coping with and assessing their own world better and better – that these same people, in the sphere of practical life decisions, will forever endure the destiny imposed on them without any attempt to reshape it?

One is indeed to assume more or less that. And, on the whole, just the opposite holds true: the spread of sport does not resolve complexes, but is among other things a symptom of repression on a grand scale; it does not promote the reshaping of social relations, but all in all is a major means of depoliticization. Which does not mean that the exaggerated importance of sport may not also express the revolutionary mass yearning for a natural law to be erected against the ravages of civilization. It is not just because of the many lakes that water sports are so popular in Berlin. Thousands of young employees dream about canoeing, and the Müllers alluded to in the *Uhu* 'Ramble' mentioned earlier forswore every other pleasure for the sake of their sailing-boat. 'The boat is just everything to us, even our summer holiday.' The naked body evolves into the symbol of the human individual liberated from prevailing social conditions, and to water is ascribed the mythic power to wash away the dirt of the workplace. It is the hydraulic pressure of the economic system that overcrowds our swimming baths. But in reality the water just cleanses the bodies.

In the Luna Park, of an evening, a fountain is sometimes displayed illuminated by Bengal lights. Cones of red, yellow and green light, continually re-created, flee into the darkness. When the splendour is gone, it turns out to have come from the wretched, cartilaginous structure of a few little pipes. The fountain resembles the life of many employees. From its wretchedness it escapes into distraction, lets itself be illuminated with Bengal lights and, unmindful of its origin, dissolves into the nocturnal void.

# Seen from above

'One of the qualities ... that contemporary employers still lack to a regrettable degree', director Karl Lange declares in a recently delivered lecture 'Economic Democracy as Organized Economic Freedom' (issue 12 of the journal *Maschinenbau*, 20 June 1929), 'is self-confidence – by which I mean not personal pride of the individual, but self-confidence of the employer class as such.' Lange defined the confidence he demanded as a 'self-confidence founded upon an ideology'. 'Without such an ideological foundation', he said, 'no group can hold its ground in public struggle today.' If we adopt Lange's terminology, it may be added that absence of ideological foundation affects the position not just of the employers, but also of the salariat. For the life of salaried employees desperately needs some adequate explanation for the constraint that weighs upon it; and the more the ruling class dispenses with the proper concepts, the more this life will lose its way. Muteness up above plants confusion down below.

There is no lack of arguments for free private economy. The employers, for their part, dispute that at the present stage it still squanders economic energies anarchically. They assert, on the basis of examples and counter-examples, that it enables economic productivity to increase as no other system does. They ascribe to it alone the ability constantly to raise the condition of the working classes. It is not a matter here of debating these certainly very important arguments; the question is rather whether they provide the ideological foundation asserted to be necessary by Lange. The indispensable precondition for private economy is the autonomous entrepreneur, so the defence of his sovereignty is the central issue. 'There can ... be no doubt', says Lange, 'that capitalist economy owes its immense economic successes, and the tempestuous pace of its development, to free competition: to the rivalry among countless autonomous entrepreneurs, whose economic existence depends upon the success or failure of their enterprises.' By what motives is the entrepreneur guided?

According to the conventional dogma, the collective interest is less the motive than the result of his actions. First and foremost he must possess the qualities that will help him to victory in the competitive struggle – which, it is claimed, will automatically bring about the material (hence, according to an implicit conviction, also the ideal) advancement of the masses. No wonder profit-seeking is given a positive sign. As has been assumed since time immemorial, it serves the general interest at the same time as it pursues selfish ends. Other crucial entrepreneurial qualities are initiative and self-reliance; to which may perhaps be added pleasure in one's own creative capacity and economic power.

The survival of the present system, which is regarded as the best, is thus founded upon certain natural qualities of its ruling stratum; not, however, upon the express will of this stratum to satisfy the demands of the masses. Therefore, one of the most common objections to planned economy, as it is characterized in the book *Wirtschaftsdemokratie* ['Economic democracy'] edited by Fritz Naphtali, is that it dethrones the entrepreneur and so strives to organize what can be achieved only through free competition. An attempt is made to prove that today's corporations, in so far as they are not monopoly cartels, restrict themselves to organizing economic freedom; that they not only represent no approximation to planned economy, but on the contrary should be viewed as a developmental phase of undiminished capitalism. The bureaucratization connected with planned economy is primarily held responsible for the inhibition of economic productivity which is to be expected. Indeed, it is already the case with existing concerns that they have to struggle against the danger of bureaucratization; and the works-council chairman of one big firm does not hesitate to tell me that, due to an excess of organization, the bureaucracy in his enterprise forms a single, inert mass. This is not to accept that such deformations are necessary under all circumstances. Organizational arrangements that in the present context engender a crippling bureaucratization do not have to stifle élan in an existence subject to other laws.

All arguments in favour of the prevailing economic system are based on belief in a preordained harmony. According to them, free competition by itself generates an order that cannot be conjured up by reason; the entrepreneur's profit-seeking, initiative and self-reliance by themselves guarantee the prosperity of the masses better than any will directed towards this prosperity. One may strive to derive the economic virtues of the present system from experience, one may try to show in detail how the entrepreneur's profit-seeking combined with competition guarantees the optimal social product – the arguments adduced do not suffice for the desired ideological foundation of the preordained harmony between natural entrepreneurial qualities and a truly valid order. Such a foundation, however, is all the more necessary since this harmony is supposed to be asserted and pitted against socialist convictions. The gap that opens here is not merely not filled: filling it is emphatically refused. 'It is just as an outstanding political economist (Böhm-Bawerk) once said', comments Adolf Weber in his book *Ende des Kapitalismus?* (Max Hueber, Munich), 'in economic life actions are more far-reaching than the ideas of the actors; economic reason makes use as it were of human desires and impulses, even human weaknesses, in order to cope with economic necessities.' But precisely in that case it is absolutely inadmissible to console oneself with a reason ruling above people's heads whose cunning evidently far surpasses the Hegelian kind. Certainly instinct and intuition grasp what is accessible only later to consciousness; this does not at all mean, however, that construction of the economic system must from the outset refuse legitimation through consciousness – let alone that any human weaknesses are especially called upon to realize it as if while sleepwalking. To renounce explaining such wonderful harmony is no ideological interpretation, but a symptom of repression. Such a renunciation would at best be understandable if the tragic divergence between human desires and human well-being were to be shown and bottomless pessimism resisted closing the abyss. But what is at stake is the same preordained harmony whose secular confidence was once based, gloomily but magnificently, on Puritanism's doctrine of predestination. Laissez-faire, laissez-aller still just sufficed for ideological embellishment of the entrepreneurial personality; yet by now even trust in time-honoured individualism has disappeared. As Lange at least says, in the lecture mentioned earlier: 'To those who advocate the idea of socialization through planned economy, one cannot really dispute that, as things are today, a complete return to a purely atomistic and individualistic liberalism is no longer conceivable.'

That trust has undoubtedly been shaken by the persistent strength of socialism, which has thereby scored a victory in the enemy camp itself. Entrepreneurs are at any rate so overwhelmed by socialist objectives that they endeavour to graft them on to their own. Arguments endowing the entrepreneur with the capacity to bring about general prosperity, by virtue of purposes quite unconcerned with the prosperity of the masses, are supplemented by explanations that further elevate the entrepreneur – unconsciously following his bent – to being the bearer of the right social outlook. Not that such arguments are not made in good faith; but they do not develop coherently from the logic of capitalism. For if profit-seeking or pleasure in economic power count as guarantees of order, a social outlook, however conciliatory its intentions, is a bonus suspended ideologically in the void. It cannot be claimed on the basis of capitalist assumptions, but is on the contrary a concession to the employees. That it is not obligatory is proved by the fact it is quite often forsworn in the competitive struggle with more primitive capitalist desires. Better suited to these desires than an addition of humane feelings is the widespread theory that enterprise as such is an end in itself. Its transfiguration is indeed the only way of releasing the entrepreneur's sovereignty from the sphere of subjective claims to power and basing it on an objective condition. Thanks to the doctrine of the supremacy of enterprise, he seemingly becomes dependent upon something higher; he becomes the servant of his work just as the King of Prussia was the servant of the state. In his article 'Probleme des lebenden Aktienrechts' ['Problems of current share law'] Oskar Netter, echoing Rathenau, champions the proposition that 'enterprise as such' has in principle been accepted as established law; an assertion that is no less instructive for lacking general acknowledgement. But what is 'enterprise as such'? Is it really something higher in which even the individual will of the entrepreneur is absorbed? If that were so, then the enterprise could not be extolled as 'enterprise as such', but would have to include a designation identifying its purpose. Works may be good or bad, may harbour a social outlook or exclude one. The work as such is a concept without content, which precisely through its emptiness proves that it merely reflects the entrepreneur's sovereignty in the objective sphere, without subordinating this sovereignty to anything higher. Even if one replaces the entrepreneur by the enterprise, there is no warrant for any belief in harmony between that enterprise and the desired social construction. The *Werksgemeinschaft* is admittedly supposed to represent the accord between work and community. Yet in it, as has been shown, work does not serve the idea of community, but rather community serves the accumulation of power of an undefined work. That the *Werksgemeinschaft* does not really imply the development of true human relations is quite correctly emphasized by Hans Bechly of the Deutschnationale Handlungsgehilfen-Verband, in his lecture 'The Question of Leadership in Germany Today' – even if his criticism is necessarily sustained by the inherently dubious concept of the organic national community. Bechly explains:

> The *Werksgemeinschaft* is supposed to become the new basis for all organic growth in both nation and state. But the firm has meanwhile become the germ of all materialist thought, so that – even if the entrepreneurial class still has national-educational qualities and even the moral strength to lead the nation's citizens – no national citizens, inwardly acknowledged as enjoying genuinely equal rights, are produced by this kind of *Werksgemeinschaft*. Various charitable institutions have indeed been established. But management, not leadership, of people is the final aim.

The employers frequently deplore the mistrust of their good intentions displayed by workers and salaried employees. They should not be
too surprised that the masses are suspicious. This does not at all stem
solely from political or trade-union influences; rather, its deeper cause
lies in the feeling of those below that leadership is indeed not the final
aim of the ruling stratum. The employers' arguments forfeit their
powers of attraction precisely because they relinquish the advent of a
proper human order to the automatic course of free competition. The
human is thus not intended, but arises at best as a side-effect; so in truth
it cannot even arise, since it must be addressed in order to be capable
of responding. This is the real complaint against today's economy: that
it does not function for the sake of the masses who work in it, but at
best manages them. In a recent issue of the *Borsig-Zeitung*, a hospital
worker expresses in his own way what the lower classes expect of their
leaders: 'We must be shown justice by those above us, offered a good,
shining example and a moral support to which we can cling.' It is dark
up above, those at the top do not shine.

The blame for this is hard to apportion, and at any rate lies only
partly with the employers themselves. During the post-war period they
not merely had to find their way in altered social and economic
conditions, they were also saddled with the demand that they fill the
vacuum left behind by the vanished former upper class. The task of
leading instead of simply managing fell to them overnight. They try to
master it by transforming the old form of rule into an enlightened
despotism that makes concessions to the socialist counter-current; but
the problems of such a solution are revealed by the very lack of self-
confidence that Lange denounces. How hard-won even these exceptional concessions have been, I know from the youngish personnel
manager of one big firm: an honest-minded person, who revealed to
me that although his older fellow directors do under the pressure of
circumstances give him a free hand, for their own part they are unable
to abandon their *Herr-im-Haus* [master-in-the-house] standpoint. All the
compromises prove only, of course, that for the sake of the sovereign
economy the employers are adapting to present conditions – but
without basing themselves upon them. A stratum thus finds itself in
power which, in the interest of power and at the same time against this
interest, cannot found its own position ideologically. But if it shrinks
itself from confronting the reason for its existence, the everyday life of
the employees is more than ever abandoned.

For some time now in Germany, especially in Berlin, a young, radical
intelligentsia has developed that in journals and books comes out quite

vigorously and uniformly against capitalism. To the superficial glance it seems to be a serious opponent of all powers that do not, like itself, strive directly for a reasonable human order. But even if its protests may be sincere and often fruitful, it makes protesting too easy for itself. For it is usually roused only by extreme cases – war, crude miscarriages of justice, the May riots,[18] etc. – without appreciating the imperceptible dreadfulness of normal existence. It is driven to the gesture of revolt not by the construction of this existence itself, but solely by its most visible emissions. Thus it does not really impinge on the core of given conditions, but confines itself to the symptoms; it castigates obvious deformations and forgets about the sequence of small events of which our normal social life consists – events as whose product those deformations can alone be understood. The radicalism of these radicals would have more weight if it really penetrated the structure of reality, instead of issuing its decrees from on high. How is everyday life to change, if even those whose vocation is to stir it up pay it no attention?

18. On 1 May 1929 the Berlin police fired on demonstrators, after which there was a crackdown on the Communist press and defence units.

# Dear colleagues, ladies and gentlemen!

'Since jobs no longer afford any pleasure nowadays', the leader of one Free employee union tells me in conversation, 'contents have to be delivered to people from elsewhere.' The same conclusion is reached by the previously cited article 'Paths to Job Satisfaction' in the GdA journal (no. 9, 1929), which explains: 'Yet the possibilities for enlivening work spiritually – and for making jobs more interesting for employees, so that they provide more inner satisfaction – are limited. Expedients must therefore be sought that can counteract the spiritual desolation of the working population.' Such expedients are seen as including art, science, radio and, of course, sport. The idea, however, that the desolation stemming from the world of work would be diminished if worthwhile contents were imparted to employees in their free time, is far from innocuous. To proceed in this way means cordoning off mechanized work like the source of an epidemic. It cannot be smothered like an epidemic, though, but on the contrary influences people even at times not devoted to it; were it to take up only five instead of eight hours, it would still be anything but a detachable function that could simply be bracketed off. Its harmful effects can be reduced not by a consciousness that looks away from it, but only by one that includes it. If, on the one hand, the trade unions advocate a rational ordering of economic life that imparts some comprehensible meaning to the individual's activity, it is not very consistent if, on the other hand, they seek to provide consciousness with contents that do not alter its relationship to mechanized work. But the contents to be imparted are also stripped of their proper sense by the purpose associated with them. They evaporate as soon as they are regarded as secure possessions, and simply used to fill people out or elevate them above their everyday existence. You must be gripped by them – and may then later also be elevated. The opinion according to which the drawbacks of mechanization can be eliminated with the help of spiritual contents administered like medicines is itself one further expression of the reification against whose effects it is directed. It is sustained by the notion that such contents represent ready-made facts, to be delivered to your home like commodities.

This is a notion that characteristically also designates contents as 'cultural goods'. As an article in the journal *Der Behörden-Angestellte* puts it, 'It cannot be doubted that the principle of freedom represents a valuable idea that is among the most precious cultural goods of mankind.' However confidently the Free employee unions and the Gewerkschaftsbund der Angestellten (the Deutschnationale Handlungs-gehilfen-Verband may be disregarded in this context, on account of its conservative corporatist ideology) patrol the area of socio-political problems, just as inconfidently do they meanwhile traverse all regions that do not directly touch upon social praxis. Here, in the true sphere of contents, the vulgar-Marxist theory of ideology takes its toll, accord-ing to which cultural contents are merely the superstructure over the particular socio-economic infrastructure; according to which, therefore, their claim to truth is not investigated at all, but merely the conditions under which they appear. The lower classes' detachment from spiritual life takes its toll – for which they themselves are assuredly least of all to be blamed. The cultural elements introduced nowadays by the unions, in order to create a counterweight to desolation, are either labelled 'cultural goods' – which are not questioned, because there is apparently nothing more to do about them – or they are scraps from the bourgeois kitchen that now end up down below at a reduced price. With the best will in the world to elevate the employees spiritually, as it were, you often fail to hit the mark. The youth groups of the ZdA (Zentralverband der Angestellten), excellently led by the way, stage 'trash-revues' dedicated to ridiculing pornography and cheap literature. Yet the *Tag des Buches* can be celebrated in the ZdA journal *Der freie Angestellte*.[19] 'We too must prepare a great success for the *Tag des Buches*. As Free trade unions we are happy to cooperate with everything that serves the spiritual advancement of the people.' Wanting to eradicate trashy literature only to be edified by the *Tag des Buches* betrays that inadequate contact with contents that does not reach the content at all. The criticism made at the time in the *Frankfurter Zeitung*, with respect to the

19. The *Tag des Buches* or 'Day of the Book' was a pseudo-educational event promoted by the government, which took place on 22 March (the anniversary of Goethe's death) and was first held in 1929. For Kracauer's scathing unsigned article on the subject, 'Für die ewig reifere Jugend. Anmerkungen zu dem erstmalig für den 22 März 1929 geplanten "Tag des Buches"' (*Frankfurter Zeitung*, 12 March 1929), see *Schriften* 5, 2 (*Aufsätze 1927–1931*), Suhrkamp Verlag, Frankfurt am Main 1990, pp. 142–6.

formality of such thought, its dubious neutrality and its purely external relationship to literature, would have become the unions better than the shallow optimism with which they greeted its blessings. The *Tag des Buches* is not merely no token of spiritual advancement, it is a greater obstacle to it than the consumption of penny shockers, which are by no means as pernicious as they would like to make young people believe. At all events, their black-and-white effects are worth more than the idylls that are cultivated right in the middle of the GdA Yearbook for German salary-earners. The latest yearbook starts off:

> Beloved and esteemed contemporary, in the present yearbook for 1929 you will once again find a section 'For Reflective Moments' – but this time I particularly want to draw your attention to it, since it contains a little sketch entitled 'Hands that Sow' by the writer Max Jungnickel. Here the writer tells of an old peasant custom. While ploughing, the farmer lets his little four-year-old daughter scatter the first golden grains of seed-corn on to the soil. 'The child walks over the ploughed clods and, with her tiny hand, clumsily throws the grains over the fresh soil!' Is that not worth reflecting upon?

What would indeed be worth reflecting upon is how one can get to the spiritual front instead of letting oneself be foddered on staple goods in the rear. So long as the employee unions do not manage to free themselves from certain prejudices adhering since the nineteenth century to a popular socialism that for a long while has not been confined purely to the socialist parties, the danger exists that the advocates of social progress will rub shoulders with unenlightened provincials, whose spiritual character is more bourgeois than the bourgeois avant-garde; in other words, they will scarcely be able to pursue their aims really wholeheartedly. Nor do the aims themselves remain unaffected by this.

Sport, free weekends and hiking – despite their neutrality, which allows them to be used for differing power objectives – impart a dignity to purely vital urges that does not fully accord with the hierarchy of values installed by the trade unions' economic programme. By seizing hold of these vital expressions, the employee unions sometimes more or less fall victim to the powers vested in them – an irresolution that is just as characteristic of their lack of definite knowledge as is their trust in the possibility of supplying cultural contents as it were from outside. In conversation with me, one works-council member defends rowing because it brings people into contact with Nature; and an article in the *Jugend-Führer* (information for the leaders of trade-union youth sections) has the presumption to assert: 'Outside in Nature's kingdom, the insanity of the capitalist mode of production in hurrying and chasing after profit becomes obvious to us.' As has already been mentioned, a supposed natural law is erected against the present-day economic system without it being realized that precisely Nature, which is also embodied in capitalistic desires, is one of that system's most powerful allies; and that its perpetual glorification, moreover, conflicts with the planned organization of economic life. The attitude embodied by the sport business leads to ideologies not in accord with the demands of the employee unions, and a movement that should be guided sweeps its conquerors away. Sometimes they even become willing vassals. In the reports of the GdA's education section, the Neumünster local branch justifies its invitation to the celebrated sportsman Dr Otto Pelzer as follows:

> The local branch committee held the view that one could best draw close to employees of younger generations, who are only feebly represented in our membership, if one responded to their overriding interest in sport and asked some particularly renowned sportsman to speak in a broad context about the connection between the sports movement and a modern employee union.

At the end of the report comes this summary: 'Everybody was talking about us, and many people will have regretted not being there on the evening of the lecture.' Such a lot going on, just so the connection will not be missed. Rather than getting to the bottom of enthusiasm for sport and perhaps restraining it, you pander to it uncritically for publicity purposes. Everybody is talking about you, but you have lost your own power of speech.

'Since, for today's working man, a collapse of psychic energies is taking place inexorably at work and on the job', writes Richard Woldt in his study 'The German Trade Unions in the Post-war Period' (see *Strukturwandlungen der deutschen Volkswirtschaft*, vol. 1), 'a collectivist association with the life of the trade unions must be achieved and maintained outside the workplace.' But a community is never formed as a substitute for the collapse of psychic energies – it consists of human individuals whose existence is crucially defined by true knowledge. Many things indicate that the employee unions tend to regard collectivism in itself as a source of their energy. I once attended the performance of a Free trade union's speech-and-movement chorus. The young people, girls and boys, with drooping arms and shoulders bemoaned their lot as slaves to the machine, then drew themselves upright and rejoiced in a kind of triumphal procession towards the realm of freedom. A spectacle whose good intention was no less moving than its aesthetic clumsiness. It was supposed to represent the community of like-minded people, but in reality expressed not so much collectivity as the will to it. This will is based on the belief that collectivity can embody, or even generate, a meaning – whereas, in reality, knowledge founds collectivity. Collectivity in itself is just as empty as enterprise in itself, and merely the opposite pole of the entrepreneur's private initiative. The position remains the same whether you approve individual initiative, in the expectation that it will guarantee general well-being, or you acknowledge the masses as a fighting community, in the hope that it will realize aims worth struggling for. In both cases, you accept people without inquiring what relationship they have to the aims in question. Now if collectivity is overstressed – and already almost posited as a content in itself – then every deviation from it, every human expression that does not lead to community as such, must be excommunicated. But since dependants today are moulded by circumstances, this simply means making a virtue out of the need for standardization. The human individual, who confronts death alone, is not submerged in the collectivity striving to elevate itself into a final purpose. He is formed not by community as such but by knowledge, from which community too may arise. The doctrinaire attitude with which the employee unions frequently fail to meet human reality indirectly confirms that collectivity as such is a false construction. What matters is not that institutions are changed, what matters is that human individuals change institutions.

# Appendices

# A

# 'An outsider attracts attention'
## – on *The Salaried Masses* by S. Kracauer

*Walter Benjamin*

Very ancient, perhaps as old as literature itself, is the literary type of the malcontent. Homer's backbiter Thersites, the first, second and third conspirators of Shakespeare's royal dramas, and the grumbler from the one great play of the World War,[20] are so many changing incarnations of this single form. But the literary renown of the species does not seem to have emboldened its living exemplars. They usually pass anonymously and taciturnly through life, and for physiognomists it is a real event if one of the clan some day draws attention to himself and declares in public that he is not playing along any more. Even the individual we are concerned with here admittedly does not quite do so by name. A laconic S. before the surname warns us against jumping to any hasty conclusions about his appearance. In a different way, the reader encounters this laconicism within: as birth of humanity from the spirit of irony. S. takes a look into the courtrooms of the Labour Court and even here 'the merciless light ... really reveals not wretched people, but conditions that make people wretched'. One thing at least is clear. This man is no longer playing along. Refusing to mask himself for the carnival that his fellow men are staging – he has even left the sociologist's doctoral cap at home – he elbows his way boorishly through the crowd, here and there lifting the mask of someone particularly jaunty.

Easy to understand if he protests against letting his undertaking be called a reportage. First, he finds those godfathers of reportage *neuberliner Radikalismus* and *neue Sachlichkeit* equally detestable. Second, a troublemaker lifting the mask does not like to be termed a portraitist. Exposure is this author's passion. And it is not as an orthodox Marxist, still less as a practical agitator, that he dialectically penetrates the existence of employees, but because to penetrate dialectically means: to

20. Karl Kraus's *The Last Days of Mankind.*

expose. Marx said that social being determines consciousness, but at the same time that only in a classless society will consciousness become appropriate to that being. It follows that social being in the class state is inhuman in so far as the consciousness of the different classes cannot correspond to them appropriately, but only in a very mediated, inauthentic and displaced fashion. And since such false conscious-ness results, among the lower classes, from the interests of the upper, among the upper classes from the contradictions of their economic position, the production of a proper consciousness – and precisely first among the lower classes, who have everything to expect from it – is the primary task of Marxism. In this sense, and initially only in this, does the author think in a Marxist way. His very project, though, leads him all the deeper into the overall structure of Marxism because the ideology of salaried employees, via memory- and wish-images from the bourgeoisie, represents a unique superimposition upon given economic reality that comes very close to that of the proletariat. There is no class today whose thinking and feeling is more alienated from the concrete reality of its everyday existence than the salariat. And what this means, in other words, is that accommodation to the degrading and inhumane side of the present order has progressed further among salaried employees than among wage workers. Their more indirect relation to the production process finds its counterpart in a far more direct involvement in the very forms of interpersonal relation which find their counterpart in this production process. And since organization is the actual medium in which the reification of personal relations takes place – also the only one, incidentally, in which it could be overcome – the author necessarily arrives at a critique of trade unionism.

This critique has to do neither with party politics nor with wage policy. It is also not so much demonstrated by one passage as discernible in all. Kracauer's concern is not with what the union does for employ-ees. He asks: How does it train them? What does it do to liberate them from the spell of ideologies that fetter them? In answering these questions, his consistent role as outsider serves him well. He is bound to nothing at all that authorities might invoke in order to call him to order. The idea of community? He exposes it as a variety of opportun-ism designed to secure economic peace. The superior education of salaried employees? He calls it illusory and demonstrates how helpless the employee is rendered in defending his rights by extravagant educational pretensions. Cultural goods? Concentrating on them, in his view, means encouraging the notion according to which 'the drawbacks of mechanization can be eliminated with the help of spiritual contents administered like medicines'. This whole ideological construct 'is itself one further expression of the reification against whose effects it is directed. It is sustained by the notion that such contents represent ready-made facts, to be delivered to your home like commodities.' Sentences like this express not just an attitude to a problem. Rather, this whole book has become a grappling with a section of everyday life, an inhabited Here and lived Now. Reality is so greatly neglected that it must show its colours and name names.

The name is Berlin, which for the author is the city of employees *par excellence*; so much so that he is absolutely aware of having made an important contribution to the physiology of the capital. 'Berlin today is a city with a pronounced employee culture: i.e. a culture made by employees for employees and seen by most employees as a culture. Only in Berlin, where links to roots and the soil are so reduced that weekend outings can become the height of fashion, may the reality of salaried employees be grasped.' The weekend is also the province of sport. The critique of enthusiasm for sports among employees shows how little the author is disposed to compensate for his ironic treatment of the cultural ideals of the *bien pensants* by an all the more fervent profession of faith in nature – far from it. The mistrust of instinct fostered by the ruling class is here countered precisely by the writer as protector of unspoiled social instincts. He has remembered his strength, which consists in seeing through bourgeois ideologies, if not completely, at least wherever they are still associated with the petite bourgeoisie. 'The spread of sport', Kracauer says, 'does not resolve complexes, but is among other things a symptom of repression on a grand scale; it does not promote the reshaping of social relations, but all in all is a major means of depoliticization.' And still more decisively in another passage: 'A supposed natural law is erected against the present-day economic system without it being realized that precisely Nature, which is also embodied in capitalistic desires, is one of that system's most powerful allies; and that its perpetual glorification, moreover, conflicts with the planned organization of economic life.' In line with this hostility to Nature, the author precisely denounces 'Nature' where conventional sociology would speak of degenerations. For him a certain traveller in tobacco products, the personification of jauntiness and worldly wisdom, is Nature. It is hardly necessary to point out that in so consistent a thinking through of economics, which exposes the primitive not to say barbaric character of relations of production and exchange even in their contemporary abstract forms, the notorious mechanization takes on a very different emphasis than it has for social pastors. How much more promising, to this observer, is the soulless mechanized motion of the unskilled worker, than the thoroughly organic 'moral pinkness' that, according to the priceless formulation of one personnel manager, is supposed to indicate the complexion of the good employee. 'Moral pinkness' – so that is the colour shown by the reality of employee existence.

The personnel manager's figure of speech shows to what extent employees' slang communicates with the author's language; what agreement there is between this outsider and the language of the collective at which he has taken aim. We learn quite automatically what blood-oranges, cyclists, slime-trumpets and princesses are. And the more closely we become acquainted with all this, the more we see how knowledge and humanity have taken refuge in nicknames and meta-phors, in order to avoid the pompous vocabulary of trade-union secretaries and professors. Or, in all the articles on imbuing wage labour with fresh, more spiritual and deeper values, is it a matter less of vocabulary than of a perversion of language itself, which covers the shabbiest reality with the most intimate word, the vilest with the most refined, the most hostile with the most peaceable? However that may be, in Kracauer's analyses, especially of Taylorist academic expertise, there are elements of the lively satire that has long since withdrawn from the realm of political caricature in order to claim an epic scope corresponding to the immeasurability of its subject. This immeasurabil-ity, alas, is desolation. And the more thoroughly it is repressed from the consciousness of the strata overcome by it, the more creative it proves to be – according to the law of repression – in the production of images. The processes whereby an unbearably tense economic situation pro-duces a false consciousness may easily be compared with those that lead neurotics or psychotics from unendurably tense private conflicts to their own false consciousness. So long, at least, as the Marxist theory of superstructures is not supplemented by its urgently needed counterpart concerning the genesis of false consciousness, it will hardly be possible to answer otherwise than in terms of the model of repression the question: How can the contradictions of an economic situation engen-der a consciousness inappropriate to it? The products of false conscious-ness are like picture-puzzles, in which the main thing just barely peeps forth from clouds, leaves and shadows. And the author has descended to the advertisements in employee newspapers, in order to detect the main things that appear puzzlingly embedded in the phantasmagoria of glamour and youth, culture and personality: namely, encyclopaedias and beds, crêpe soles, anti-cramp pens and quality pianos, rejuvenation elixirs and white teeth. But in time something higher, not content with a phantasy existence, inserts itself into the everyday life of the firm just as puzzlingly as wretchedness does into the glamour of distraction. Thus Kracauer recognizes in neo-paternalist office management, which ulti-mately amounts to unpaid overtime, the model of the mechanical organ from which long-forgotten echoes arise; and in the dexterity of the shorthand typist the petit-bourgeois desolation of the piano étude. The authentic symbolic centres of this world are the 'pleasure barracks': stone, or rather plaster, incarnations of the employees' pipedream. In exploring these 'shelters for the homeless', the author's dreamlike language displays all its subtlety. Astonishing how flexibly it moulds itself to all these atmospheric artists' cellars, all these tranquil Alcazars, all these intimate coffee-nooks, in order to cast them as so many tumours and abscesses and expose them to the light of reason. *Wunderkind* and *enfant terrible* in one person, the author here tells tales out of the school of dreams. And he is far too knowing to consider such institutions as mere instruments of stultification in the interest of the ruling class, or to make the latter solely responsible for them. However trenchant his critique of employers may be, considered as a class they partake too strongly of the subaltern character of their subordinates, in his view, to be acknowledged as an authentic moving force and autonomous actor amid the economic chaos.

This essay will have to dispense with any political effect in today's terms – i.e. any demagogic effect – not merely because of such an assessment of employers. Consciousness, not to say self-consciousness, of this sheds light on the author's distaste for all that has to do with reportage and *die neue Sachlichkeit*. This left-radical school may conduct itself as it likes, it can never eliminate the fact that even proletarianization of the intellectual almost never creates a proletarian. Why? Because from childhood on the bourgeois class has provided him with a means of production in the shape of education that makes him identify with the bourgeoisie – and perhaps even more the bourgeoisie with him – on the basis of educational privilege. In the foreground this solidarity may become effaced or even dissolve; but it almost always remains strong enough to exclude intellectuals from the constant state of alert, the front-line existence, of the genuine proletarian. Kracauer has taken these perceptions seriously. Which is why his essay, by contrast with the radical fashion-products of the latest school, is a landmark on the road to a politicization of the intelligentsia. There, a horror of theory and knowledge that recommends them to the sensation-seeking of snobs; here, a constructive theoretical training that is addressed neither to the snob nor to the worker – but that is instead capable of producing something real and demonstrable: namely, the politicization of its own class. This indirect effect is the only one that a revolutionary writer from the bourgeois class can resolve upon today. Direct effectiveness can emerge only from praxis. But he, unlike more successful colleagues, will be mindful of Lenin, whose writings best show how far removed is the literary value of political praxis, its direct effect, from the junk of raw facts and reporting that passes for it today.

So by right this author stands there at the end – all alone. A malcontent, not a leader. Not a founder, but a spoilsport. And if we wish to visualize him just for himself, in the solitude of his craft and his endeavour, we see: a ragpicker at daybreak, lancing with his stick scraps of language and tatters of speech in order to throw them into his cart, grumblingly, stubbornly, somewhat the worse for drink, and not without now and again letting one or other of these faded calicoes – 'humanity', 'inner nature', 'enrichment' – flutter ironically in the dawn breeze. A ragpicker at daybreak – in the dawn of the day of revolution.

# B

# Chronology

1889    Siegfried Kracauer is born on 8 February in Frankfurt am Main. He is the only child of Rosette and Adolf Kracauer.

1898    Attends grammar school.

1904    Switches over to the Klinger–Oberrealschule.

1907    Kracauer passes his exams and leaves school. In August his first contribution to the features pages of the *Frankfurter Zeitung* appears. He takes up the study of architecture at the technical college in Darmstadt.

1908–09    Continues his study of architecture at the technical college in Berlin, and completes his diploma at the technical college in Munich.

1911    Employed by an architectural practice. Travels, writes literature and prepares his dissertation on *The Development of Wrought-iron work in Berlin, Potsdam and Several Other Towns in the Region from the Seventeenth to the Early Nineteenth Century.*

1914    Dissertation accepted in Berlin and published in 1915 by the Worms Verlags- und Druckereigesellschaft. Returns to Frankfurt when war breaks out. Works for an architectural practice.

1916    Participates in a competition to design a war cemetery, and wins. Gets to know Max Scheler.

1917    Called up to join artillery in Mainz.

1918    Takes up position as an architect in Osnabrück. Death of father. Return to Frankfurt. Alongside 'bread and butter' work, engages in the study of philosophy and writing. Family encourages him to make friends with Theodor W. Adorno (born 1903). In 1920 he will meet Leo Löwenthal.

1919    Writes a study of his teacher from the Berlin days: *Georg Simmel. A Contribution to the Interpretation of Contemporary Mental Life.*

1920–22   After occasional work as an architect and at the *Frankfurter Zeitung*, he becomes a salaried writer at the newspaper in 1921. From now on, many of his important essays find their first appearance here. Makes acquaintance of Rabbi Nobel and Franz Rosenzweig.

1922      *Sociology as Science* appears. Begins his study of the *Detective Story*. Travels with friends Adorno and Löwenthal. Meets Bloch, but contact is broken off for several years after Kracauer's critical review of Bloch's book on Thomas Münzer.

1924      In November Kracauer becomes a full editor at the *Frankfurter Zeitung*.

1925      Begins work on the novel *Ginster*.

1926      Kracauer meets Elizabeth (Lili) Ehrenreich, the woman who will later become his wife. She works as a librarian at the Institute for Social Research. She stems from a Catholic family in Strasbourg and studied music and art history. Criticism of Buber–Rosenzweig translation of the Old Testament leads to a regrouping in his circle of friends (reconciliation with Bloch, splits from Buber and Margarete Susman). First essays on film appear.

1927      *The Mass Ornament* and the essay on *Photography* are published. Trips to Paris and France.

1928      The novel *Ginster* appears, first in extract form in the *Frankfurter Zeitung*, and is later published by S. Fischer.

1929      Begins work on a new novel, *Georg*, which he completes later in exile. Pre-publication of one chapter. *Die Angestellten* appears in twelve instalments in the newspaper, and is finally put out by the Frankfurt Societäts-Druckerei.

1930      Kracauer and Lili Ehrenreich marry and move to Berlin, where Kracauer joins the Berlin bureau of the *Frankfurter Zeitung*.

1931–33   Relations between the Berlin editorial staff deteriorate dramatically. Conspicuously anti-semitic feelings sour the atmosphere, while, at the same time, the financial situation worsens. Kracauer's pay is drastically reduced. Redundancies are frequent. Kracauer wages a campaign against Ufa (the state film conglomerate) in the press, attacking its production of ever more nationalistic films. On 28 February 1933, one day after the Reichstag fire, the Kracauers leave for Paris. Kracauer is promised a position as foreign correspondent for the *Frankfurter Zeitung*. This does not come about. The newspaper drops him like a hot potato.

1933    A difficult period in exile in Paris is marked by competition for journalistic assignments and for work with the old friends from Frankfurt. Contact with Walter Benjamin.

1934    Kracauer finishes his novel *Georg*. After that he begins work on the Offenbach book.

1935    Offenbach study is completed. The publication of *Georg* is delayed. The Offenbach project draws some sharp criticisms from Adorno.

1936–39    Small commissions from New York from the New School for Social Research and the Institute for Social Research. Prepares to emigrate to US. Finally takes the necessary affidavit. Gets an offer to write a social history of German film for the Library of the Museum of Modern Art. This project eventually turns into *From Caligari to Hitler*. Once war breaks out Kracauer is interned for two months in the vicinity of Paris, along with other emigrants from Germany. Various advocates successfully push for his release. Emigration proves to be more difficult than expected.

1940    Interned once more and released. A daring escape attempt leads him to Marseilles where he meets up with Benjamin once more. Difficulties on the Franco-Spanish border, which lead to Benjamin's suicide in September, seem insurmountable.

1941    Successful crossing of Spain to Portugal. More difficulties in Lisbon. At the end of April Lili and Siegfried Kracauer eventually reach New York.

1941–45    Once there he takes up a post as Iris Barry's assistant at the Library of the Museum of Modern Art and starts work on *From Caligari to Hitler*. The next few years are taken up with various commissions, amongst these the study of *Propaganda and the Nazi War Film* and *The Conquest of Europe on the Screen. The Nazi Newsreel 1939–1940*. These studies tend to be empirically based, particularly the analysis of filmic material.

1946    The Kracauers become American citizens.

1947    On Erwin Panofsky's recommendation, Princeton University Press publishes *From Caligari to Hitler*.

1949    Aided by a stipend, Kracauer commences work on *Theory of Film*. Notes from the period spent in Marseilles form its underpinning. Explores psychology.

1950    Undertakes commissions for the *Voice of America*. Parallel to his work on the aesthetics of film, Kracauer turns himself into a expert in empirical social research.

1951    He becomes Director of Research in the Department of

Empirical Social Research at Columbia University. Works together with Lazarsfeld.

1952    His essay on *Qualitative Content Analysis* is published. The years until 1955 are completely taken up with empirical studies and the organization of research.

1956    Takes up the work on *Theory of Film* once more.

1959    Completes *Theory of Film.* While working on the book, he visits Europe for the first time since the end of the war, and undertakes other empirical studies.

1960    The plan of the history book emerges, but the book itself will remain a fragment. In the following years Kracauer is kept busy by trips to Europe and various new editions of his rather dispersed writings, translated into various languages.

1966    In the final year of his life Kracauer spends the summer months in Europe. Once back in New York he falls ill and succumbs to pneumonia on 26 November.

# Bibliography

## I. Single works

*Die Entwicklung der Schmiedekunst in Berlin, Potsdam und einigen Städten der Mark vom 17. Jahrhundert bis zum Beginn des 19. Jahrhunderts*, Wormser Verlags- und Druckerei GmbH, Worms 1915.

*Soziologie als Wissenschaft. Eine erkenntnistheoretische Untersuchung*, Sibyllen-Verlag, Dresden 1922. Second edition in S.K., *Schriften* 1, Suhrkamp, Frankfurt am Main 1971.

(Anonymous) *Ginster. Von ihm selbst geschrieben*, S. Fischer, Berlin 1928. Translated into French. Second edition *Ginster* (without the final chapter), Bibliothek Suhrkamp, Frankfurt am Main 1963.

*Die Angestellten. Aus dem neuesten Deutschland*, first and second editions Societäts-Verlag, Frankfurt am Main 1930. Translated into Czech. Third edition Verlag für Demoskopie, Allensbach and Bonn 1959. Fourth edition (pirated, without author's preface), Berlin 1970. Fifth edition in S.K., *Schriften* 1, Suhrkamp, Frankfurt am Main 1971. Sixth edition (under licence) Gustav Kiepenheuer Verlag, Leipzig and Weimar 1981, afterword by Lothar Bisky.

*Jacques Offenbach und das Paris seiner Zeit*, Allert de Lange, Amsterdam 1937. Translated into English, French and Swedish. Second edition as *Pariser Leben. Jacques Offenbach und seine Zeit. Eine Gesellschaftsbiographie*, List, Munich 1962. Third edition Deutsche Buchgemeinschaft, Berlin 1964.

*Propaganda and the Nazi War Film*, Museum of Modern Art Film Library, New York 1942.

*The Conquest of Europe on the Screen. The Nazi Newsreel 1939–1940*, Library of Congress, Washington DC 1943.

*From Caligari to Hitler. A Psychological History of the German Film*, Princeton University Press, Princeton NJ 1967. Translated into French, Italian, Polish, Spanish. German version (much shortened): *Von Caligari bis*

*Hitler. Ein Beitrag zur Geschichte des deutschen Films,* Rowohlt, Hamburg 1958.

(with P. L. Berkman) *Satellite Mentality. Political Attitudes and Propaganda Susceptibilities of Non-Communists in Hungary, Poland and Czechoslovakia,* Praeger, New York 1956.

*Theory of Film. The Redemption of Physical Reality,* Princeton University Press, Princeton NJ 1997. Translated into Italian. German translation under author's supervision: *Theorie des Films. Die Errettung der äusseren Wirklichkeit,* Suhrkamp, Frankfurt am Main 1964.

*Das Ornament der Masse,* essays 1920–1931, Suhrkamp, Frankfurt am Main 1963. Translated into English as *The Mass Ornament. Weimar Essays,* translated, edited and with an introduction by Thomas Y. Levin, Harvard University Press, Cambridge Mass. and London 1995.

*Strassen in Berlin und anderswo,* essays from the *Frankfurter Zeitung* 1925–1933, Suhrkamp, Frankfurt am Main 1964.

*History. The Last Things Before the Last,* Markus Wiener Publications, 1995. German translation: *Geschichte. Vor den letzten Dingen,* Suhrkamp, Frankfurt am Main 1971, as fourth volume of *Schriften.*

*Der Detektiv-Roman. Ein philosophischer Traktat* (1922–1925), first published in S.K., *Schriften* 1, Suhrkamp, Frankfurt am Main 1971.

*Ginster* (full version), *Georg* (first edition), in *Schriften* 8, Suhrkamp, Frankfurt am Main 1973.

## II. Numerous essays in periodicals

*Logos, Neue Rundschau, Preussische Jahrbücher, Frankfurter Zeitung, Neue Zürcher Zeitung, Mercure de France, Figaro, Revue Internationale de Filmologie, Penguin Film Review, Magazine of Art, Social Research, Partisan Review, Commentary, The New Republic, Sight and Sound, Public Opinion Quarterly, Political Science Quarterly, Saturday Review, Kenyon Review, New York Times Book Review, Theatre Arts, Filmkritik.*

## III. Secondary sources

*Permanent Exiles. Essays on the Intellectual Migration from Germany to America,* Martin Jay. (See in particular chapter 11, 'The Exterritorial Life of Siegfried Kracauer'; chapter 12, 'Politics of Translation: Siegfried Kracauer and Walter Benjamin on the Buber–Rosenzweig Bible'; and chapter 13, 'Adorno and Kracauer: Notes on a Troubled Friendship'.)

*Fragments of Modernity: Theories of Modernity in the Work of Simmel, Kracauer and Benjamin,* David Frisby, MIT Press, 1988.

*Critical Realism: History, Photography and the Work of Siegfried Kracauer,* Dagmar Barnouw, Johns Hopkins University Press, 1994.

*New German Critique* no. 54, Fall 1991 (special issue on Siegfried Kracauer).

# Translator's note

Apart from the general difficulty of doing justice to the wide range of stylistic registers exploited by Siegfried Kracauer, the translator of *Die Angestellten* is confronted by one immediate problem to which there is no wholly satisfactory solution: namely, the title and subject of the work. The problem arises because specific German social legislation has given far sharper definition to categories that in English remain approximate and essentially descriptive. For this reason I have felt compelled to adopt the admittedly rather ponderous and foreign-sounding salaried employee/employee/salariat group of renderings. I should have done so, moreover, even were such alternatives as white-collar worker (a 'common but absolutely meaningless term': Harry Braverman), clerk, clerical worker or office worker not ruled out by other considerations – as being too gender-specific, too dated, too restrictive, etc.

I have usually followed the conventional practice of retaining the original names of trade union journals, but append below their English versions.

It remains only to thank those who have provided invaluable help in the preparation of this translation. Nick Jacobs and John Willett were unstinting with their time and knowledge in tracking down cultural allusions. Martina Dervis showed exemplary patience in answering a host of stylistic and linguistic queries. Above all, Inka Mülder-Bach meticulously read the entire translation in draft and contributed many felicitous suggestions for improvement. I am deeply grateful to them all, although responsibility for the final result is naturally my own.

*Afa–Bundeszeitung = Afa–Bund* newspaper
*Allgemeine Deutsche Gewerkschaftsbund* = Confederation [literally General Union] of German Trade Unions

*Allgemeine Freie Angestelltenbund (Afa–Bund)* = General Free* Employees' Union

*Allgemeine Verband der Deutschen Bankangestellten* = General Association of German Bank Employees

*Allgemeine Verband der Versicherungsangestellten* = General Association of Insurance Employees

*Bund der technischen Angestellten und Beamten (Butab)* = Union of Technical Employees and Officials

*Der freie Angestellte* = The Free Salaried Employee

*Deutsche Werkmeisterverband* = German Foremen's Association

*Deutsche Gewerkschaftsring* = German Trade-union Ring

*Deutsche Bankbeamtenverein* = German Association of Bank Officials

*Deutschnationale Handlungsgehilfen-Verband* (DHV) = German National Association of Shop Assistants

*Gesamtverband Deutscher Angestelltengewerkschaften (Gedag)* = Confederation of German Employee Unions

*Gewerkschaftlichen Aufklärungsblätter* = Trade-union Education Papers

*Gewerkschaftsbund der Angestellten* (GDA) = Associated Union of Employees

*Grundriss der Sozialökonomik* = Outline of Social Economics

*Hirsch–Dunckersche Gewerkverein* = Hirsch–Duncker Company Union

*Maschinenbau* = Mechanical Engineering

*Reichsausschuss werksgemeinschaftlicher Verbände* = National Board of Company Community Associations

*Reichsausschuss werksgemeinschaftlicher Verbände* = National Board of Company Community Associations

*Reichsbund Deutscher Angestellten–Berufsverbände* = National Union of German Professional Associations for Salaried Employees

*Verband der weiblichen Handels- und Büroangestellten* = Association of Female Shop and Office Employees

*Vereinigung der leitenden Angestellten (Vela)* = Union of Managerial Employees

*Zentralverband der Angestellten* (ZdA) = Central Association of Salaried Employees

---

* From the last decade of the nineteenth century, trade unions in Germany were divided into two broad currents: the Free, socialist in orientation, and the Christian Social.